CREATING THE GOOD LIFE

A Practical Guide to Personal and Financial Happiness

By K. Thomas Decoster, CFP®

There are simple steps that anyone can take to create a life filled with the maximum amount of opportunities for happiness every day.

This book is a key for the door to that pathway.

ISBN-10: 1478321830
EAN-13: 9781478321835

Dedication

Of all the lessons I have learned since leaving home at age eighteen to earn my doctorate in the school of hard knocks, few have exceeded the lessons in life that I learned from my Dad.

He taught me that in order to have what you want, you must first be willing to give something in return. "The Lord helps those who help themselves." Being proactive was simply one of his unstated, basic principles of life.

He taught me that the more you try, the greater your chances are of success. If you do not try, you have no chance.

He taught me that it is better to give a 100% effort once than it is to give a lesser effort two or three times.

He taught me that you can learn to speak two languages fluently, even if you only have a third-grade education. He taught me that no one stops you, unless you stop yourself.

He taught me that if you consistently give people more than they expect of you, you will never be without friends or employment.

He taught me, "A fool and his money are soon parted." Never risk your money on things you do not understand.

He taught me not to judge people or situations too quickly, in spite of rumors or reputation.

He taught me tolerance and compassion for others by the way he treated strangers as well as friends.

He taught me to be happy with simple things.

He taught me about the rhythms of nature and how to live off the land without malice or guilt.

Of all the things I learned in his presence, however, I am most thankful for the fact that he taught me by example to expect to succeed in whatever you attempt to do. You have little to lose and everything to gain. In our home, I have no recollection of failure ever being discussed.

My father was not a perfect man, and he did not speak with eloquence or flair. He was a simple man who taught these important lessons by living a life of hard work, fairness to others, and positive expectations in everything he did.

This book is a tribute to those lessons in a form that, hopefully, my children, grandchildren, and others will find helpful in achieving a happier life.

Contents

Acknowledgments

The information contained in this short book is the result of more than seventy years of life, an unquenchable thirst for knowledge, and over twenty-five years of work as a Certified Financial Planner.

No small handful of individuals I might name, or a collection of experiences I could mention, could ever adequately acknowledge the depth and breadth of the help I have received.

I owe much to, literally, hundreds of authors and the books I have read on the subjects of wealth management and human behavioral psychology. They deserve my sincere thanks and great praise for the wisdom they have shared. They have also provided me with many of the quotes that have become the guiding principles in my life.

I also thank each member of my family. They have tolerated all the late work nights throughout the years, as well as all of the ups and downs that a career in financial planning brings. I especially wish to thank my wonderful wife, Callie, who helps me keep the balance that is so vital to a truly successful life.

Preface

Change is Difficult

As I recall from my high school physics class, "A body in motion tends to stay in motion. A body at rest tends to stay at rest." At that time, I thought this was only a physics lesson. Much later in life, I learned that these natural laws apply to human attitudes and habits as well. In fact, psychologists tell us that one of the most difficult things to do in life is change. An estimated 98% of everything we do every day are deeply entrenched habits. In spite of this fact, a small percentage of ordinary people, most having no unusual or remarkable natural talents, still manage to accomplish extraordinary things every day. I'd like to see that percentage increase. This book is about what it takes to make that happen, while enjoying the process at the same time.

In that regard, I am reminded of the story of the man who prayed to God each day to win a million-dollar lottery. After many months passed without winning a single dime, he threatened God that he would never go to church again if he did not win the very next lottery. He concluded that another failure to win was clear evidence that there was obviously no God to hear his prayers. He suddenly heard a voice boom from the heavens above, "You could at least buy a ticket."

Congratulations! You have already learned that one of the secrets to success first requires that you buy a ticket. No amount of thinking and wishing will bring success without effort. I know that whoever you are, it is your sincere desire for positive change that has brought you to this book. You have already separated yourself from much of the pack. I commend you on the efforts already undertaken in your life's journey to get you to this point. You are now about to begin another great adventure.

It is a well-researched and astonishing fact that only 10% of people who start reading a book like this ever read past the first chapter.

This book is designed to give you a clear strategy to help you win the game of success. The more concepts you learn and apply, the greater the chances are that you will be a winner today and in the future. If you do not read this entire book, your future accomplishments will surely be minimized because it is clear that you are not really dedicated to changing your future by exploring the many practical options that can create positive change.

The ideas within this book do not belong to me or to any one individual. They belong to thousands of authors from the past and to the individuals who have been willing to adopt and adapt them in order to create more successful daily attitudes and habits. It is my fondest hope that once you have experienced the power held within these ideas, that you, too, will feel compelled to share them with others.

You are about to begin a great adventure. In order to follow those who have traveled these pathways before you, it is necessary to accept the challenges ahead with the same spirit of adventure others have successfully embraced. In order to succeed, you must also be willing to use the ideas you learn even before you fully grasp or appreciate their full significance and power.

You must also have faith in yourself and your ability to become more than you now are. Faith allows you to begin with enthusiasm. Your confidence and full belief in the ability of these techniques to change your life for the better can only happen later, as positive experiences fortify your new-found wisdom.

There really are secrets to living your life better. The fact that you are reading this book tells me that you already know some of them. I am sure there are some you use regularly. I also know from experience that you have probably also forgotten many of them. There are also techniques you once heard about, but never got around to using. This book is designed to reintroduce ideas you already know, combined with others you are not yet aware of, with a specific method that allows you to be able to remember and incorporate them into your life as positive, life-long beliefs, attitudes, and habits.

I have had the great fortune in life to be blessed with both personal happiness and financial success beyond my wildest dreams, but things did not happen magically over night. I therefore truly appreciate the time you will take in allowing me the opportunity to share the secrets of that success with you.

For more than fifty years, I have worked diligently to absorb and adapt the lessons within hundreds of books on the subjects of behavioral psychology and personal success. Attempting to cover the immense volume of knowledge encompassing all human emotional experiences is an impossible task, to say the least. Therefore, the choices selected within this book are, of necessity, arbitrary. Because of the breadth of the subject matter contained in this book, by design, there are many omissions of important subjects. I can only hope I have covered those that you will find the most important and meaningful to your success.

Within my personal and professional life, my challenge has been to sort through the confusion and distill my lifetime of experience and knowledge into concise lessons and wisdom, which can be shared with others in order to help with making the best possible choices along the many pathways of their lives. This book is a continuation of that effort.

Knowledge is important; however, knowledge alone is not enough. It is the willingness to take the actions necessary that will ultimately change habits, apply knowledge gained, and then to continually make fine adjustments along the way. Those are the things that will keep you on the path of personal and financial success. Hopefully, you will find this book helpful and stimulating enough to give you the extra boost necessary to break free of some of your less effective habits, and thereafter continue, for a lifetime, with new habits and methods absorbed by applying what you have learned.

While each chapter is not designed to be an exhaustive study of each topic, my hope is that you will find the distillation of years of study and research presented within this book to be sufficiently detailed enough to provoke you into taking action. It is only then that you will obtain the concise insight, a perspective of persistent optimism, and the wisdom necessary to achieve a more balanced and successful life.

One critical lesson for achieving this success is avoiding procrastination. So, let's begin. I wish you well.

Enjoy your journey.

Chapter 1

Happiness

The very purpose of life is to seek happiness.
—His Holiness, the Dalai Lama

The very nature of our being is to continually seek something better than we already have. The persistent motion of our lives flows naturally toward the pursuit of happiness and away from pain and suffering. It drives every action in our lives.

Everyone's ultimate goal, at life's most basic level, is to experience a relatively constant state of happiness and fulfillment rather than pain. If that is true, then why do so many live with far too many days of unfulfilled happiness? The answer is quite simple: Comprehensive lessons for leading a happy life are rarely taught, and when they are, they are usually buried in one or more subplots. In the pages that follow, I hope to do my small part to help change that.

The struggle for a secure, fulfilling life is an ongoing need we must all deal with, in one way or another. The difference between those who look back on life and see it with the pride of accomplishment

1

and satisfaction, and those who see it with regret, lies primarily in the lessons we learn, the attitudes we maintain and the beliefs that guide our lives. It is the actions those lessons and beliefs prompt or discourage that make all the difference.

No one would deny the advantage of superior intellect, physical attractiveness, being born to the right parents, or occasional good luck. Yet, it is not infrequently the case that those with the most inherent advantages are not the most successful—measured by either wealth or happiness. That is because each of us is propelled along life's path only in part by our genetic make-up or by good luck.

One of mankind's greatest discoveries is that if we can change the focus of our thinking, we can change our destiny.

The socially-conditioned and self-induced programming we allow our brains to focus on most of the time is ultimately the most important factor in determining whether we succeed or fail.

The word "happy" is derived from the Icelandic word, *happ*, meaning luck or chance. Although many people believe good luck is the source of happiness, lasting happiness is never merely a matter of chance. Even if you have the good fortune to be luckier than most, this fact alone does not guarantee a happy life. The good news is that, with proper training and practice, you can learn to live your life every day with a far greater sense of fulfillment, a higher degree of serenity, and a lasting happiness.

Some may say, "You just don't understand my situation. It's not that easy to be happy." I am painfully aware that sadness is as much a part of life as happiness. Statistics on national health estimate that as many as one in five Americans suffer from dark moods that sometimes deepen and linger for days, weeks, or months. For many, the chance of that condition leading to clinical depression is a real threat. Modern medication and/or psychotherapy can and does help many of these individuals. In fact, if you are having deeply depressing thoughts, feelings of suicide or your depression is chronic and persistently interferes with your job and family relationships, you should seek help immediately.

Chronic depression is very treatable with both medication and therapy. However, such treatments are usually only part of the solution. Most individuals who suffer from lingering sadness or depression have also developed deeply ingrained habit patterns of depression. Those habits make future depression a self-fulfilling prophecy. I do not take lightly the fact that this cycle of depression can be very difficult to overcome. For many, however, overcoming those habits can be accomplished to a very significant degree by learning how to diminish negative thoughts and beliefs and systematically replacing them with the attitudes and patterns of optimistic expectations. Let's start right now.

If you currently feel too depressed to start the process of change right now, try this: Find something other than yourself to think about. Focus your thoughts upon someone less fortunate than yourself, and think about what you might be able to do to help.

The average life expectancy for someone born between 1990 and 1995, living in 29 of Africa's poorest countries, is currently 45 years of age. In Mozambique, it is only 39.2 years. The average life expectancy in the United States is currently 78.3 years, and increasing annually. In fact, the number of U.S. residents aged 90 or older has nearly tripled since 1980, to 1.9 million, and is projected to reach 8.7 million by mid-century.

We can certainly all be grateful to live in a country where civil wars, disease and lack of a daily meal doesn't lead to the likelihood of a dramatically shortened lifespan. Perhaps you could make a small donation to help feed at least one starving child through the Feed the Children organization. Helping others is feel good medicine for both the giver and the receiver. (*www.feedthechildren.org*).

Having a persistent attitude of gratitude for all the obvious blessings surrounding you every day is also a great start to eliminating more than a small portion of the depressing feelings and thoughts that regularly drag you down. Since gratitude is such a good creator of happier feelings, the only question one should now ask is "How can I use this information to my best advantage?"

Here is your answer; if you want to feel happier every day, just complete this easy 3 minute exercise before going to bed each evening.

On a pad of paper write three sentences that state, "I am grateful for _____because_____".

Now fill in the blanks with three specific and different things to be grateful for each day.

Your gratitude may be for something as simple as a sugar cookie or as grand as your grandchildren. Every time you do this simple gratitude exercise in the future you are guaranteed to receive a subtle and automatic happiness lift.

Each day look for three new and different things to write on your list. When you start to think about things to be grateful for during each day simply because you know that you need to have a list of three new and different things to write down at the end of each day, your gratitude awareness is going to be automatically raised. Sooner than you would imagine, you will learn that appreciation for what you already have is a skill worth honing. Learning how to focus daily on an attitude of gratitude can change your whole life. This is a skill that, with practice, can become a priceless habit. Gratitude is one of life's most important cornerstones. If you will continue to do this simple 3 minute exercise for 60 days it is highly likely to become a life changing habit. Can you spare 3 minutes a day to permanently change your life for the better?

HAPPINESS CREATION

> *The mind is its own place, and in itself can make*
> *a heaven of hell, a hell of heaven*
> —John Milton

While some pursue happiness, others create it. We cannot change others or events beyond our control. However, like the gratitude exercise, with practice, we can change our attitudes, expectations, and actions, and those are the things that make the real difference between living a life of regret and living a life of happiness.

> *Life is only 10% about what happens to you, and 90%*
> *about what you think and do about what happens to you.*

To have a wonderful life, it is tremendously helpful to have wonderful days. In order to have wonderful days, you will benefit greatly by repeatedly focusing your thoughts on all of the positive possibilities and not the problems strewn throughout each day. This perpetually optimistic way of thinking is not something most people are born with. If it is not something you have already learned from your parents or peers, it is something that you can learn with practice until you become a happier you.

The two distinguishing characteristics of individuals who achieve lifetime joy and a passion for living are that they have a purpose they pursue and the knowledge that they control their future. They constantly apply themselves in ways that consistently bring more and more success into every aspect of their life. They understand that there *are* answers to just about everything they are willing to pursue. They believe that their dreams have a very good chance of being attained to the extent that they are willing to search out the answers and apply what they learn.

If your most wished-for dream is now being lived by others, but not by you, it is most likely because those individuals have simply taken control over the direction of their life, and you have not.

If the answer is that easy, then why don't more people take control? The short answer is because they don't believe they can. They don't believe they can because they don't know how. The longer answer is that there are, indeed, many obstacles that can block the way. Some are obvious, but many are not. The obstacles that are not clearly obvious are often the ones that become insurmountable.

HAPPINESS STARTS WITH YOU

Only you can identify the specific causes for suffering and happiness in your life. You might start your search by first sitting down with paper and a pen and listing everything you think makes you unhappy. Next to each item on this list, write down the part you play—large or small—in the creation and continuance of these unhappy circumstances. If you cannot find any part you play in your own unhappiness, I suggest you give each of these items a lot more thought. The purpose of this exercise is simply to help you recognize that the causes of at least some of your unhappiness begins and ends in your own thoughts and actions. When you accept responsibility for at least some contribution to your own unhappiness, you will have made a significant breakthrough in your quest for greater happiness because if you acknowledge that you are creating some of your own problems you can also acknowledge that you also have the opportunity to eliminate some or all of this self-destructive behavior..

When you change your attitude, your whole world changes

Please don't tell me that "A leopard can't change its spots." The part about the leopard may be true, but when it comes to you, I strongly disagree. You can change. It is simply a matter of sustained desire and applying a few simple activities that work better and better the more you practice them. My life's experience and the experience of millions of others just like me is a living testimony to that fact. The libraries of this world are filled with their autobiographies and histories. Through honest self-examination, greater self-awareness, and specific action, you can change. You can be happier than you now are. The evidence of this fact is overwhelming.

THE PATH TO GREATER HAPPINESS

As you age, you will surely change. The only question you must answer is, "Do you want to control the direction of that change, or do you prefer to just sit back and take whatever you get, by chance?"

Several years ago, Duke University did a study on "Peace of Mind." They found that the following factors were the greatest contributing factors in creating a general feeling of happiness. These are all attributes you can achieve by your own effort and design. First you must choose to do so.

1. The absence of suspicion and resentment.
2. Forgiveness of yourself and others is essential to happiness. Carrying around a grudge or guilt is a major cause of unhappiness. Learn to forgive and forget.
3. Not living in the past. Preoccupation with old failures and mistakes fosters and promotes depression. Look to the future.
4. Stop wasting time and effort on things you cannot change. If you can't change it, let it go. Move on with positive things you can change.
5. Stay involved with the living world. Resist the temptation to withdraw or become reclusive during periods of emotional stress. Seek support from others.
6. Refuse to indulge in self-pity when life hands you a raw deal. Accept the fact that nobody gets through life without some degree of misfortune and suffering.
7. Cultivate the old-fashioned values of love, honor, compassion, and loyalty.

If you find little or no similarity between the list above and your life, clearly some change is needed if you are to experience greater happiness. Don't expect too much of yourself in the short run. When the gap between your expectations and your achievements is too wide, feelings of inadequacy are inevitable. (Higher, long-term goals are fine to have, and are strongly encouraged.)

HAPPINESS IS A CHOICE

The fountain of content must spring up in the mind. And he who hath so little knowledge of human nature as to seek happiness by changing anything but his own disposition, will waste his life in fruitless efforts and multiply the grief he proposes to remove.
—Samuel Johnson

We all have pain and suffering of some kind in our lives. The idea that you can choose to achieve and maintain a greater level of happiness does not contradiction the fact that various, unpredictable events have a role to play in your happiness or emotional pain. Family, friends, lovers, and others, over whom we may have little or no control, always manage to inflict some of this suffering upon us. You cannot hope to control all of life's uncertainties or what others choose to do or not do. Such events, and what others do, have the potential to create situations, with or without intention, that can be emotionally painful. Nonetheless, the degree to which you experience happiness or pain still depends upon how you think about those actions and how you choose to respond.

There are many levels of pain and suffering we can control. Unhappiness is not an all or nothing kind of switch, one we switch either on or off. On a scale of one to ten, you may feel an unhappiness level of eight in a situation that many others would only respond to with an unhappiness level of four or five. You might argue that your response is not controllable.

There are many opinions regarding the degree to which individual biochemistry and factors of environmental adaptation govern the outcome of our overall happiness. Many researchers argue for a preset biological happiness factor that is genetically wired into our system from birth which cannot be changed.

Past research has shown strong evidence that demonstrates that different individuals have very different degrees of left (positive/happy) and right (negative/unhappy) prefrontal cortex activity, which may be genetic in nature. Therefore, each of us has a biological bias for either more or less natural happiness.

These studies also indicate that sustained emotional stress floods the brain with cortisol, the master stress hormone, which in turn damages the left (positive/happy) prefrontal cortex area of the brain, particularly in young children. Severe stress can affect the size of the structures in the brain, cause cell death, and also affect the number of connections between brain cells.

It is believed that lack of love, comfort, and security may have lasting effects on the prefrontal cortex, and that this stress may eventually even lead to clinical depression. However, your natural bias and/or stress are not the only factors that count. Recreational drug users will tell you that they also know more than a few ways to induce pleasure and suffering.

However, more recent brain research demonstrates that happiness can be created by stimulating the left prefrontal cortex. In fact, in more recent happiness research, it has been learned that the brain has much greater neuroplasticity than previously recognized. The brain can permanently increase the pleasure centers activity and area by introduction of happiness producing activities and habits.

Whatever the baseline may be for each individual's level of happiness, the search for truth does not stop here. There is also no disagreement regarding the fact that our attitudes and thoughts are also very capable of changing, to a remarkable degree, the biochemistry of our bodies, and therefore our happiness.

Even the prefrontal cortex researchers note that patients can use neuro-feedback to induce more positive states of mind and emotional well-being. One researcher notes, for example, that the left cortex produces positive feelings simply by having a person set a simple goal—such as leaving the house before seven in the morning—and then accomplishing that goal.

It is clear that we are able to change our body's chemistry dramatically from moment to moment simply by changing our thoughts. If you have any doubts about that, just wait until you feel the sudden surge of anger you get the next time someone rudely cuts you off in traffic.

If we choose to think and act in certain ways, greater happiness can certainly be one of the results. When done frequently enough, greater happiness can become a permanent change; therefore, happiness is, to a significant extent, a choice.

HAPPINESS IS AN INSIDE JOB.

Unless you are stimulating your mind with drugs or other artificial forms of stimulation, happiness is always connected to your own thought processes. Although the things most frequently pointed out as the sources of happiness are external, those things are usually just events of temporary pleasure.

Not money or cars, jewels of kings, the homes of millionaires, soul mates to fill your heart's desire, or any other person, can make you happy or give you happiness. The material things of life give you momentary pleasure, but that temporary pleasure almost never translates into lasting happiness.

Studies of lottery winners who win millions, and studies of individuals who recently suffered grave physical injuries or illnesses, clearly demonstrate that each of us has a kind of built-in happiness thermostat. We can be easily elated or depressed by one or more of life's unexpected events, but following a reasonable adjustment period, all human beings tend to gravitate back to their original level of happiness or suffering. This information supports findings of the prefrontal cortex researchers previously mentioned. That is because pleasure and happiness are two very different things.

We can engage in many activities that bring us momentary pleasure, but eventually lead to suffering rather than happiness. Recreational drug use and marital infidelities are two examples of activities that bring some individual pleasure, but not happiness. Lady luck may reward us with unexpected fortunes of one sort or another to brighten our day, but even those pleasurable events will not give us lasting happiness.

> *Happiness does not depend on what we have;*
> *it depends upon who we are or become.*

Although constant higher levels of lasting happiness may seem a goal out of reach for the average individual, it is possible to achieve higher levels of happiness and contentment much more of the time than most people have come to believe. The only requirement to reach this goal is to learn and adopt a few simple attitudes and actions in daily life.

First, you must be willing to acknowledge that finding and maintaining greater happiness is your own responsibility. It can never be a task delegated to outside events or individuals.

THE HAPPINESS TEST

Think about your past, and recall a wonderful experience you have had. Choose one that gave you unforgettable pleasure and joy. Close your eyes and vividly imagine, in great detail, the past moment of great joy you selected. Try to relive the joy you felt at that moment in time.

If you are unable to think of anything at this moment, use food, as in the following example.

Vividly imagine that you are eating your favorite, juicy fruit or, if you prefer, a freshly baked cinnamon roll. Imagine the terrific smell and appearance of the food before you start to bite down. Next imagine the feel of the food in your mouth and the juice that flows in your mouth from the smell and taste of the first bite. Vividly imagine the smell and wonderful flavor. Imagine every detail of the moment.

<u>Do this visualization now!</u> **It is *very important to* complete this very quick visualization exercise before you continue.**

How do you feel? Maybe hungry, but also pleasant and happy? If you conducted this little exercise correctly, you felt good, didn't you?

Now do the same, highly imaginative visualization test using another of the most pleasurable experiences you can think of from the past. Once again, see everything vividly in your mind. See the setting. Smell the smells. Be there fully in that moment for at least thirty seconds. Then, come on back.

***STOP READING!!!** It is extremely important that you do not proceed before doing this visual exercise first.*

Welcome back. Erase those pleasant thoughts and try another quick exercise.

For the next visualization, think back to a terrible, emotionally painful, experience from your past. Perhaps it is the death of a loved one or a public humiliation or a severe injury. If you are fortunate as to not be able to think of something this distressing, visualize a person you would say you most dislike.

Now, dwell for a moment on this person, time of distress or extremely painful experience from your past. Pick something that was a very distressing and intense experience for you; something that hurt you deeply. Perhaps it is something that you are still deeply angry or hurt about.

Go back in time to the day of the event. Think about what occurred just before this experience took place. Picture where you were. Were you alone or with someone? Close your eyes and experience it all again in your mind. Mentally relive this event in the greatest visual details and emotions possible. Stop whenever you've had enough of this distasteful exercise.

You were no longer filled with the feelings of joy or happiness, were you? Were your teeth clenched? Were any of your muscles tight? Is there still a furrow in your brow? Do you now wear an intense look on your face?

Now erase those thoughts and mentally move on to another location: the neutral ground of rational thinking.
You have just taken a trip. If you actually followed the instructions given above, I know you have also actually experienced both happiness and suffering which you just created all by yourself, without the help of outside events.

I cannot emphasize enough the extreme significance of this important lesson.

You have just created happiness and suffering all by yourself. You did not need anyone or anything else to help you.

The potential for happiness is a choice you can control.
Happiness primarily depends upon where you choose to focus
your attention the majority of the time.

Aside from moments when you are actually involved in an experience that creates physical pain, you can bring out the good feelings of happiness any time you want by just visualizing the same, joyful event you selected for this test or by focusing on other positive happenings and possibilities in your life. Unless you have previously had some training in hypnosis, yoga, meditation, or some other form of inner-directional control, you can't possibly know the power you have to control your physical and mental well-being. Even pain can be greatly modified, and often completely eliminated, through the use of mental exercises you can learn. Only you can stop "you" from making the choice of happiness. That is why you often hear the quote, "Attitude is everything." It is not the events in our lives that control happiness, but rather our attitudes following each good or bad event.

I am reminded of the Zen story of a man chased by a hungry bear over the edge of a cliff. After jumping, he manages to grasp a small bush growing ten feet down from the top of the cliff, and three hundred feet above the cliff's floor. As the roots of bush begin to pull loose, he notices a beautiful, red strawberry growing within the delicate green leaves of a strawberry plant growing on the cliff's face, and within his reach. He plucks the berry, pops it into his mouth, and bites down to savor its sweet juices the same moment the roots of the bush pull loose from the face of the cliff, and he falls to his ultimate death. As he falls, he exclaims, "What a delicious strawberry."

How nice it would be if all of us could adopt this Zen secret of living in the present, focusing our attention upon the ever-abundant good options life presents us with. It may be impossible for the average person to enjoy them all, but it is indeed possible to enjoy more than we now do. It is within our human capacity to exercise our ability to focus our attention upon the good things in life, thereby creating and experiencing joy during almost every moment that comprises the substance of our lives.

Happiness is not the result of a lack of conflict in our lives, but rather the ability to successfully cope with the conflicts we find unavoidably deposited upon our doorstep. It is also not a mental state we suddenly arrive at. It is the mental manner in which we choose to travel.

Since happiness is a mental state, you make it possible just about as often and as continuously as you decide, and are limited only by your understanding and utilization of success cycle methods and self-mastery lessons in the chapters that follow.

THE CYCLE OF HAPPINESS AND SUCCESS

Desire, vision, belief, attitude, action, spaced repetition, self-affirmations, habit, results, self-esteem, self-confidence, and adjustments that bring us back to the beginning with renewed and increased desire; these are the critical elements that drive the cycle of happiness and success. Each element in this cycle may rightly be viewed as a spoke in the wheel of progress that continually rolls forward along the pathway of happiness and success. This cycle carries you as far as you would like to go.

From this point forward, please understand that when I use the term *success*, it is not intended to mean personal achievement alone. Since my definition of success incorporates both happiness and self-fulfillment as necessary ingredients, you can correctly presume happiness is incorporated in every discussion of success.

Now for the good news: Once you put the cycle of success into motion, it is relatively easy to keep the momentum going in the direction of your dreams. Additionally, with each complete rotation of this cycle, just like a snowball rolling downhill, the wheel of success continually builds up, layer upon layer, positive experiences. These results allow you to move forward easier, faster, and further with every rotation of this cycle of experience. As you experience this continual growing cycle of success, you and those around you will benefit in ways you never expected or imagined possible. Many doors of possibility will open themselves to you in ways you cannot now imagine. That is because you are absorbing the skills and qualities necessary to become unbelievably happy and successful.

People enjoy being around and helping people they like. Everyone enjoys including happy people in their group. People are ten times as likely to do business with people they like, even if they may not have "the best deal in town." Happiness and success are often closely intertwined in good life experience.

Just like the snowball rolling down a long, steep hill, you, too, can start from very humble beginnings and become something truly magnificent by end of your journey. Over time, and with practice, you can become unstoppable.

Seven percent of the CEOs listed in one of *Inc.* magazine's past survey of the fastest-growing 500 private companies in America had only a high school education *or less*. An additional nine percent had only two years of college *or less*. These highly successful CEOs represent only the tip of the iceberg of what is possible for those willing to follow their dreams with commitment and action. They are living proof that it's what you do with what you have that is extremely important; not just the position from which you start.

> *Only a fool learns from experience.*
> *The wise man learns from the experience of others.*
> —Chancellor Bismarck

Who could disagree with such simple wisdom? In a world where human knowledge doubles every five years, the only sure way to maximize your success is by using the collective skills of others. Another of life's fundamental rules of success is not to waste time trying to reinvent the wheel of human experience when proven role models for success already exist. If you learn to use the collective wisdom of those before you, positive change will happen for you far more quickly.

Almost everything we do in life is governed by habit. The cycle of success is all about changing some of the perspectives you have that are less helpful for you than they could be. When you accept these new perspectives, you soon establish new habits. Once these new attitudes and habits are deeply entrenched, they guarantee you to move through life on a new, empowered autopilot setting of ever-increasing success and happiness.

This process takes time and a successful method of disciplined practice. The actual time required for lasting change is much shorter and easier than you may have been led to believe, and if you think otherwise, it is only because you have previously lacked some of the information and skills you are about to learn. That is about to change.

In summary: Happiness is something you have far more control over than you have imagined in the past. You simply need a pathway to consistently follow, which allows you to experience a new appreciation of your never-ending ability to change your future circumstance by changing the focus of your daily thoughts and actions. That being the case, let's explore the guideposts on that pathway in the chapters that follow.

RECOMMENDED READING;

The Mind & the Brain: Neuroplasticity and the Power of Mental Force
– Jeffrey M. Schwartz and Sharon Begley

The Happiness Advantage
– Shawn Achor

Happier
– Tal Ben Shahar

Chapter 2

Goals

You've got to have a dream to make a dream come true.

The reason most people fail to achieve the life they want is rarely because of a lack of innate ability. Rather, it is because they lack a clear destination and necessary desire. They also often lack a clear understanding of the specific tools needed to get them there. Others fail because they simply don't believe they can make significant changes in their lives by applying new ideas and information, combined with persistent effort. That's a most unfortunate misconception. Underachieving one's potential because of failing to explore all of life's options for greater success only leads to low self-esteem, and ultimately, unhappiness. Because they do not really try hard enough, those individuals will never know how easy it is to achieve real happiness.

Most low achievers fail to realize that taking the actions necessary to make their dreams come true is always much harder to start than it is to keep going. The effort needed to succeed is not an extraordinary effort that must endure year after year. It is more like a short climb up to the crest of a hill, and then pleasantly coasting down that hill, as a journey for the rest of your life. Once you begin practicing the same habits highly successful individuals repeatedly use, everything becomes easier. Everything becomes more satisfying—*even failure*. Nevertheless, you must still find the motivation necessary to get started.

There are only two basic types of motivation in life. The first motivation is the desire to experience the joy of positive results that are received in the pursuit of pleasure. The other is the desire to avoid emotional and physical pain.

Behavioral research has repeatedly demonstrated that human beings are far more motivated by pain than they will ever be by pleasure. Therefore, if you are at least a little dissatisfied with your current level of happiness or success, it is good. If you are extremely dissatisfied, that is even better. I assume you are not fully satisfied with every aspect of your life at this time. If you were, you wouldn't be reading this book. Let's focus on that for a bit. Look back over your last ten years and ask yourself a couple of questions.

1. Have you accomplished all the things you want and are capable of?
2. Have you allowed being too busy with the mundane, day-to-day chores of life suck most of the enthusiasm and passion out of your life?
3. Have you been majoring in minor things?
4. If you accumulate the same amount of wealth in the next ten years as you have in the last ten years, will you feel proud of yourself or disappointed?
5. Are your relationships with those you care about as good as you would like them to be?
6. Are you satisfied with the rate of progress you are making in pursuit of your dreams?
7. If you looked back ten years from today, and realized that you did nothing except let ten precious years of life slip through your fingers, how would you feel at that point in time?

8. Do others treat you with the love, respect and appreciation you believe you deserve?

The more disappointed you are at this moment with the life you have created, *the better your chances are for dramatic improvement.* Conversely, no matter how much you have accomplished so far in life, you can do better. There is always room for improvement.

> **The two greatest enemies of becoming your best are accepting average and good enough.**

One necessary ingredient for progress is dissatisfaction with the status quo. The greater your degree of dissatisfaction, the greater your desire will be to actually take action to help create productive change. *With persistent action, anything is possible.*

> **If you are not now achieving what you want in life, it is because you do not have clearly defined, written goals and a sincere desire to achieve them. There are no other reasons.**
> —Paul J. Meyer.

It is impossible to over-emphasize the truth contained within this famous quote. The power of setting down specific goals in writing is probably the least understood and appreciated factor in a life destined for success or for failure. Make no mistake about it: If you choose to have written goals as a guide to your future destinations, it will have the same effect as adding a turbocharger to your car's engine. You're going to find yourself propelled in a straight line, directly toward your most important goals, at a rate of speed you cannot now imagine.

Conversely, if you are not making progress each day toward some worthwhile goal, you are, by default, on the path toward a life of mediocrity at best, or perhaps much worse. Time will tell.

People don't plan to fail. They fail to plan.
A life without goals is like a ship without a rudder.

These old clichés are often heard and too often ignored. Without goals, you cannot live life fully. Every breeze that blows, and every tide that flows, carries you in a different direction. You will, in effect, forfeit one of the key elements of happiness. That element is having a purposeful life.

Life without a purpose cannot help but be filled with confusion, apathy, and dissatisfaction. The evidence is all around us. Just look through the pages of your local paper, or tune in to the nightly news. I never cease to be amazed at the number of people in trouble. These are people who have little or no directional control in their lives, and absolutely no idea how to lead a successful life.

The good news is that you need not count yourself among them. If you choose to be the captain of your own ship, to set your own destinations, to chart your own course, to steer against the tide and wind that accompanies every life, you are almost certain to reach every important destination you choose. You may arrive more quickly or later than you expect, but you will most likely arrive very close to the exact spot you imagined in your mind.

The laws of success are not based upon your opinion,
but on fundamental truths.

Quite some time ago, a startling fact was discovered while surveying the success rate of a class of students who graduated from Harvard University twenty years earlier. It was discovered that just 3% of these former students had accumulated more wealth than the remaining 97% combined!

Further investigation revealed that this astonishingly successful 3% had one important factor in common: At the time of graduation, each of these special students had specific, written goals and some sort of written action plan for their future.

This study does not surprise very many in the financial planning community, but it is often overlooked by otherwise intelligent individuals. This management by objective approach is widely recognized as the method of choice for successful business owners everywhere in the world. Yet, most individuals—and yes, even most business owners—never use this technique in their personal lives.

The power of this concept is shamefully under-utilized, simply because so few realize the incredible power it holds. The magic that a set of clear destinations brings to your life is more powerful than you can imagine. The study of thousands of individuals who came from humble beginnings, and who later achieved fantastic success in every way, is living proof of that fact.

This does not mean the path will be unrealistically easy. "Easy" is a relatively term. The more you enjoy doing something, the easier it seems. If you are doing what you love, doing it is a lot more like play than work. Even if you are not doing what you love, it usually becomes much easier over time because you become more and more skillful at the things you choose to do. Hard work can become pleasurable if you get great satisfaction out of hard-earned accomplishments. Easy or not, having highly desired goals to shoot for dramatically increases your odds of ending up in the top 3% in life, rather than never achieving your dreams.

As a bonus, this method can be applied to anything you consider important to a happy and successful life. Contrary to what many people mistakenly choose to believe, this *management by objective* concept is not just about money. It is about vision, passion, clear direction, and persistence. Each of these elements is a necessary ingredient in any plan for success. It is also not about sudden or great victories; it is about continuous, small victories that become great victories over time.

One of the keys to success in this process is not to be lured into the delusion that you can generalize your hopes and dreams because you can't seem to think of carefully defined, specific goals you want to accomplish.

In order to maintain the persistence necessary to succeed, it is absolutely critical that you write down, with great clarity, exactly what you want to achieve. Statements such as being rich, being a better person, or being successful, are not enough. You must write down exactly what each goal means to you in terms that can be measured and communicated easily to others. If your goals are unclear, your results will be as well.

Let me suggest that you go about this process as follows:

Find a quiet room where you can be undisturbed for at least an hour. Make sure to have two full pads of paper, and a good pen (or pencils) before you start.

Divide the first writing pad into six sections, with four blank pages per section. Give those six sections the following titles: "Health"; "Wealth"; "Relationships"; "Adventure"; "Legacy"; and "Personal Achievements."

Fill in each of the six sections with everything you even remotely think you would like to do or become during the rest of your life, in each of these areas of your life. In this first stage of dreaming about the future, you will need to suspend critical judgment regarding what you think you can accomplish. Your hopes and dreams are not about that. At this point, take my word for the fact that you can accomplish far more than you think you can. Trust me.

Under each topic, list *everything related to that topic you can think of* that you might like to have or become in your wildest dreams. Imagine that this is a speed writing contest. Don't dwell on every thought—; just write down as many things as you can think of as fast as you can. This list is about the dreams of your life, and not your limitations, so don't hold anything back. After you think you are finished, go back over each section; take your time. Pretend that if it's not on this list and you think of it later in life, you can't have it. It's now or never—so take your time.

If you have any problems thinking of what to write down, use these thoughts to prime the pump before you start or after you finish.

Health: What kind of physical and mental shape do you want to be in one year from today? Five years from today? How about the last five years of life?

Wealth: How much money do you want? What do you want it for? Who do you want it for? When do you need it?

Relationships: List the names of those you care about. What improvements or changes would you like to see take place? Who would you like to meet that you haven't met yet?

Adventure: What places would you like to see? What adventures would you like to experience? What challenges would you like to complete successfully?

Legacy: After you are gone, how would you like to be remembered? Who would you like to help? How would you like to help? If you could return after your death to read your epitaph, what would you want it to say?

Personal Achievements: What skills would you like to acquire? Who would you like to become? What job would you like to have? What habits would you like to develop or overcome?

Now take the second pad of paper and divide each page into three equal columns down the entire length of the page. Title the first column "Goal." Title the second "Benefit." Title the third column "Cost of Failure."

Go back to your first pad of paper and rearrange each goal you listed in the section titled, "Health" in order of importance. Give it a number. (By the way, don't even think of substituting anyone else's priorities for your own. Other people's goals and priorities are meaningless for you, unless they are also your goals.) Go back and rearrange each of the other goals in each section in priority order as well. After you have finished numbering each of the goals in each topic section, transpose each goal, in priority order, onto pad number two, in the appropriate section.

As you transpose each goal, visualize the end result for each goal in the greatest detail possible. See it. Taste it. Smell it. Look at the result as an independent observer might, and write down exactly what you see, in specific detail. Pay special attention to visualizing the details of what failure to achieve your goals will actually mean to you and those you want to love and support.

Your subconscious mind needs a crystal clear picture of the result you want to achieve. As you write out each goal, remember this:

A fuzzy goal can only give you a fuzzy result.

This is a great time to get excited. It is the beginning of a great adventure, and you're going to be the leading character in the story. Imagine, for just a moment, you have arrived at each of the destinations you chose. Suspend any doubts you may have for just a few moments.

I promise; this won't hurt. It's going to feel good. Remember our little exercise from Chapter One with creating happiness and sadness by using visualization in our minds? Take a couple of minutes right now to close your eyes and visualize being at the moment in time when you achieve success with each of your most important goals.

Take a moment to visualize just one goal that is most important for you to reach in the future. Now imagine you have arrived at the point in time, with this goal fully achieved. When you arrive there, you are thrilled. You're excited. You'll want to tell everybody about this. You have done it. You have reached your goal. Feel the joy, pride, and satisfaction. You set a goal that you weren't really sure you could accomplish, but you actually did it. As you reach each of these goals you set for yourself, you will find that they are some of the best events in your life because you—and you alone—are responsible for setting the goals and leading yourself to success.

Get excited. Excitement creates energy. Mental states change physical states. Your heart rate is probably increasing right now! Excitement stimulates activities that lead to the legendary energy of high achievers. High energy comes from passion and excitement. You're going to be energized by this process.

Anytime you feel you need a little jolt of enthusiasm, come back to this page, read it over again, and do this little mental exercise again. This is going to be fun.

For each goal you listed, I want you to now imagine that ten years have passed, and you are ten years older. In the column titled "Benefit," list the benefits you receive by reaching this goal.

In the column titled, "Cost of Failure," list the personal cost to you for failing to reach these new goals. What will your life be like ten years from today if you stay the same as you are now? How much regret will you feel? What will it cost you to decide to do nothing? What will it cost the ones you love?

Don't continue reading until you complete this exercise!

This is an appropriate time to reflect, for just a bit, on the subject of passion. No, I'm not talking about sex. I'm talking about living a life with passion. If you really don't care that much about achieving any real change in your life, I can guarantee you will never have much more than you have right now.

> *You can't amble toward success.*
> —Tony Robbins

Think and take action with eager anticipation and enthusiasm. Why choose to be less than you can be when it is so easy to become so much more? Without a passion for change, your future life will remain stuck in low gear.

There isn't any good, that I'm aware of, that comes out of apathy or lack of enthusiasm. We rob no person when we seek our own good. It does no one any good for you to remain weak, unhappy, or poor. I don't believe people are lazy. People simply have impotent goals. That's usually because they do not believe they can become much more than they currently are, or they believe it would take so much work that it isn't worth the effort. They are wrong.

WHAT'S YOUR WILDEST DREAM?

Associated Press Article:

> *A Maine-built replica of a Viking ship yesterday completed an 87-day voyage from Greenland to the New World, retracing Leif Ericson's voyage of discovery to Vineland nearly 1,000 years ago. Its 10-member crew landed this morning at L'Anse aux Meadows, the oldest known European settlement in the Americas.*

To have more, you must first become more. To become more, you must have, or create, a passion for change and passion for life. The greater your passion for change, the greater the change can be. Without passion, there will be little or no action taken by you in the direction of the new you, and not much that is new will happen. Passion is powerful. Nothing of importance is achieved without it. No matter what challenges you must face in life, if your passion is great enough, you will find a way to succeed. Put your heart and soul into even your smallest actions. That's the very essence of passion. It's another important secret of a joyful life. If you do not now have great enthusiasm regarding all the possibilities that positive changes can make in your life, don't worry, that will change. When you see the progress you are making time and time again by following the methods outlined in this book, you will become an enthusiastic believer in your own new destiny. That's the universal law of progress.

It's a sad fact of life that most people spend more time planning vacations than they do planning life itself. Don't beat yourself up about this. It's not your fault. Until now, nobody has made you fully aware of how to use these life-altering ideas. They certainly don't teach it in school. If, on the other hand, you decide that all this thinking and writing stuff is just a waste of time, then please feel free to blame yourself as much as you would like later in life.

A life by design can be an awesome thing to behold. When you complete these exercises, you will repeatedly see amazing opportunities suddenly open up in your life, just like the 3% of Harvard Graduates who left school with things they wanted written down, and a brief plan of how to get started.

Given the fact that the average life expectancy in this country is currently expanding by leaps and bounds, you may live to be 100 years old. Of the 273 million people in the United States today, about 70,000 are already age 100 or older. By the time the year

2050 rolls around, that number could be as high as 4,200,000. That fact alone certainly suggests that we make the best use of whatever years we have before us by starting right now. It also suggests that, no matter how old you are, there is still plenty of time to enjoy the results of the positive forces you put in motion today. What goal would you set for yourself today if you were convinced that you could not fail?

DEADLINES

Go back to the list of dreams and write a completion date next to each goal you are serious about.

A goal without a deadline is just an empty wish.

Without a deadline for completion, the goal is obviously something that you really don't care enough about to commit serious effort to. As with the visual picture, your subconscious mind needs clear directions regarding your time limit expectations for achieving what you want.

If you don't have a completion date in mind,
never is probably the correct date.

For goals that require several stages to complete (like becoming a world class anything), break your goal down into bit-sized steps, and give each step a deadline. Don't set out to achieve all your goals at once. That's a recipe for certain failure. Just as it is with most things in life, you need to learn to walk before you run. Write down just one or, at most, two of your highest priority goals from each category on separate, 3x5 index cards. Date the cards with the desired completion dates, and carry these cards with you every day. Read each card every morning before you start your daily chores, at mid-day, and again each night, just before you go to sleep. Do this simple task every day for the next sixty days—even if you're on vacation! Once you have built some of the habits discussed later in the book, then you can carry around as many of your goals as you want. In the beginning, though, don't overload your mind with too many things at once.

Mark a date in your calendar two months from today to review and revise the goals that didn't make it to the 3x5 cards on this first round. Review your lifetime dreams on this list at least once every sixty days for the first year. After the first year, once a year is enough, unless you prefer more often. As you achieve each goal listed on the separate 3x5 cards, save these cards to later review, reminding you of your success. As you succeed with each goal, replace the completed goal card with the next highest goal on your priority list.

RECOMMENDED READING;

Think and Grow Rich, by Napoleon Hill

Chapter 3

Obstacle Solutions

The key to happiness is having dreams.
The key to success is making dreams come true.

One might reasonably expect me to start this chapter with a list of intellectual, physical, or social handicaps that are common in our world. I could do that, but it would not help you. Most individuals find more than enough perceived handicaps without any of my help.

If, somewhere in your past, you were led to believe you have very real limits on the amount of success you can have in your life as the result of IQ tests, aptitude tests, or any other kind of peer-related test, it is time to dismiss those counterproductive beliefs right now.

Living a life of low expectations is the most certain
method for creating a self-fulfilling prophecy of failure.

The biggest obstacles you will ever need to overcome during your journey toward greater happiness and success are the self-limiting beliefs you impose upon yourself and the less-than-optimal level of self-esteem resulting from such beliefs.

Keep away from people who try to belittle your ambitions. Small people always do that, but the really great make you feel that you, too, can become great.

—Mark Twain

In my final year of high school, I was given an aptitude test. It was not something that I understood the significance of at the time. It seemed to me that the test's questions were illogical and irrelevant to anything of concern to me at age seventeen. After the test results were scored, I was called to the principal's office of our small school. The principal informed me that I had a total score of 10. I asked him what that meant. He said, "It means that you don't have enough initiative to even become a ditch digger."

I always look back on that moment with special delight every time I reach another new plateau of success in my life. I was able to do that because I knew in my heart that the test results, and the conclusions the principal drew about me, were not at all representative of the person I was or could become. However, his remarks concerned me and did not help. At seventeen, there were many things I was uncertain about in my life and in my future. Fortunately, I believed I was probably far more capable than his test score interpretation showed.

What others say to you or about you is not nearly as important as what you say to yourself.

I tell you this short story about myself not to impress you, but rather to impress upon you that no matter what someone else believes about you, the most important factor in your life is what you believe about yourself.

Your ability to succeed cannot be measured with a written exam. The factors that determine success are far more than IQ alone. Your ability to memorize textbook facts is just one element of your total skills, nothing more. It is not a measure of your ability to use your creative nature to combine all of your unique skills and talents in your own unique way to accomplish the things you feel are most important in your life. Having a good memory is a great blessing, to be sure; but that alone is not enough to assure success. The world is filled with many people with great potential and few accomplishments.

On the other hand, throughout the world, we also frequently find people like Rose Blumkin, a Russian immigrant woman who never attended school and never learned to read or write English. To make a living in her newly adopted country, she sold furniture from her basement in Omaha, Nebraska in 1937. She later put up $500 to open a small store in order to better display her merchandise. She said her business strategy was simple: "Sell cheap and tell the truth." It worked.

In 1983, after continuing to expand year after year, she sold an 80% interest in her business to the world's smartest investor, Warren Buffett, for 55 million dollars. At that time, Mrs. B, as she was affectionately called, was 90 years old. Because of her special talents with people, finance, and business, Mr. Buffett gladly kept her working within the business until her death at age 104. Warren Buffett noted, on one occasion, that "Business school students could probably learn a great deal more from watching Mrs. B for a few months than from years in graduate school."

It bears repeating: The biggest obstacles you will ever have to overcome during your journey toward greater happiness and successes are the self-limiting beliefs you impose upon yourself and the less-than-optimal level of self-esteem that results from such beliefs.

SELF-ESTEEM

One reason birds and horses are not unhappy is because
they are not trying to impress other birds and horses.
—Dale Carnegie

Self-esteem is always the direct result of comparative perfor-mance—real or imagined.

Since no one lives in this life alone, life is unavoidably a compara-tive experience. Therein lay the vast majority of all high or low self-esteem experiences and feelings. If we are guilty of social errors or other perceived self-failures, low self-esteem quickly steals our self-assurance right out from under us.

For most people, something as small as discovering we have a but-ton missing from a blouse or a stain on our clothes just prior to ar-riving at a social event, causes a very uncomfortable feeling within ourselves, or what the Japanese call "loss of face."

"Loss of face" is an interesting choice of words. Sometimes it seems that the only solution to social embarrassment is to hide our face along with the rest of our body. One very successful technique for doing this is to hide behind a reserved or shy exterior while our emotions churn on the inside. Sometimes we hide behind self-deprecating comments or jokes about ourselves. Others simply re-duce the amount of time they spend with other people to a mini-mum throughout their lives.

Each of us has a social face we put on for others. It is designed to give us a protective social barrier between the *real us* and the *social us* we wish the world to see and evaluate when compared to everyone else. The *real us* is almost never the problem. It is the comparative expectations we place upon ourselves that creates the troubling perceptions we adopt about our comparative selves. Left unchecked, these perceptions can turn an otherwise meaningful and productive life into a daily struggle to find a way to feel good about one's self.

As astonishing as it may seem, this unpleasantness can even invade the lives of some of the most successful people you know. Self-doubt does not confine itself just to the economically and socially less fortunate people among us.

The yellow pages are filled with the names of therapists trained to deal with the extreme cases of this debilitating condition. After completing the exercises suggested in this book, if you still feel crippled by self-doubt and low self-esteem, by all means, seek their help.

If, on the other hand, you find that you are able to focus in a more rational way on a few, simple global comparative facts of life, and take a few, simple action steps to progressively move you toward a better life, you may well find better places to invest your time and money than in the therapist's office.

Did you know that of 96 anti-depressant drug trials conducted between 1979 and 1996, sugar pills (placebos) often proved to be as effective as *or more effective* than the anti-depressant drugs being tested? Placebos actually changed the patient's brain chemistry and reduced clinical depression. In one test, as many as 32% of patients taking placebos reported improvement, while only 24% reported improvement with drugs such as Prozac, Zoloft, or Paxil. Expectations are powerful.

EXPECTATIONS

We only receive what we believe we deserve. For some, despite their talent and efforts, this is a real problem. Even among highly accomplished individuals, there often persists the feeling that, "Someone's going to eventually find out that I am not as good as they think I am." Self-doubt is pervasive among far too many undeserving individuals in this world. Its roots usually begin at an early age.

The world can be a very cruel place. Endlessly teasing and taunting young children can be merciless and devastating to the fragile confidence of a child. Even as we reach adolescence, we are subjected to the scrutiny of our peers. We may be labeled and scarred for life as the result of our social awkwardness or nonconforming physical attributes. Even if we are strong, these social injustices may hang on us like a great weight for the rest of our lives. For some, this weight may be so great that they eventually take their own lives.

I recognize that peer pressure will always be a very real force in every society, but if you want to find a sure path to happiness and success, first start by setting your standards higher than the small minds of thoughtless individuals.

For those who survive early childhood, there is always hope for a better life in a world that appreciates more meaningful and substantial matters of life. We don't all need to be handsome or pretty. It is not necessary to be a talented athlete or an intellectual giant. We can each create high self-esteem and satisfaction simply by becoming a good person who contributes something of value to our family, our friends, and this world. You can take comfort in the fact that there are billions of other individuals in this world just like you. They are not super human. They are still smart, funny, thoughtful, interesting, and talented—each in their own unique way.

If you do not now feel that you measure up to your peers, we need to work on that. If you are acutely aware of your faults and limitations, but not your assets, you are doing yourself and everyone around you a great disservice. Every person under the sun has unique skills and talents that are well worth exploring and expanding. You need to focus not on what others think of you, but rather on the person you would like to be. You already possess a unique list of personal assets that few, including yourself, recognize. Your job is to discover them.

I love the rhetorical question I noted on a bumper sticker one day, as I sat in my car waiting for a traffic light to change. It said, "Why be normal?" I couldn't agree more.
Being normal is about being average, which is too often about being mediocre. This life is not a dress rehearsal, and you should not be willing to settle for a mediocre experience. You should only settle for the values and goals that add meaning, pleasure, and purpose to the direction you decide to choose for your life.

A sure road to unhappiness is trying to live your life according to peer pressure, commercial advertising, or any other artificial goals that have little or no relationship to the unique person you are. There is very special level of joy that comes directly from living your life by the standards you set for yourself. That standard should be the standard of constantly striving to achieve the potential that is uniquely your own.

The secret to achieving that standard is to routinely push against the outer limits of your current self so that you may stretch your capabilities and become more than you already are. If you desire greater happiness in your life, nothing else should ever take the place of the inner competition between yourself and your potential. That is the only comparative measurement that matters. Any other comparison is irrelevant.

COMPARATIVE ANALYSIS

If you choose to live your life by constant, comparative analysis of others, you will find there is always someone who is better at doing anything you can imagine than you are. If they don't happen to live in your neighborhood, they surely live somewhere else in the world. You just haven't found them yet. That's not important. Your role in life is not to find out who is better than you at any particular thing. Your role is to find out what you are good at and take satisfaction in using your unique talents well. If you decide to use the *me versus all of the successful people in the world* analysis of self-worth, you will find it to be a guaranteed recipe for emotional disaster.

If you must use comparative self-analysis, it is wise to broaden the scope of your comparative thinking. Who are you excluding in your comparison sample? I'd like to respectfully suggest that it would be most beneficial to develop a more global view of the world and your place in it. Did you know that there are over 500,000 spinal cord disability patients in the United States? Have you considered comparing yourself to any of the unfortunate individuals born with severe mental and physical problems? Think about all of the people who end up in prison because they cannot learn to control their anti-social behavior. How do you compare to them?

If you want to feel immediately better about yourself, compare yourself to *everyone else* in the world, and not just your small circle of acquaintances or people glamorized in the news and entertainment media.

If you take a little time to look for them, you will personally find hundreds of people that have accomplished meaningful and happy lives, despite, on the surface at least, they do not appear to be either particularly smart or physically attractive. Those people have their stories told in the news we read or see every single day. In fact, they are everywhere; you just need to look for them. They are very much like you, and if they can be happy and successful, believe me—you can as well. The only difference is that they are not focused on their shortcomings and weaknesses. They are far more focused on their strengths and the many other things to be grateful about.

LEARNED HELPLESSNESS

Many years ago, behavioral researchers at the University of Michigan conducted an interesting study. They placed a Northern Pike in a fish tank with a school of baitfish. Unlike the pike's natural habitat, this particular fish tank had a sheet of glass inserted between the pike and the baitfish sections of the tank. As expected, the pike repeatedly tried to attack the baitfish and repeatedly failed, as he crashed into the glass. He finally stopped trying. The researchers then changed the rules of the game. After a few days, the glass separating the two sections of the tank was removed. The baitfish and the pike swam freely together without any attempt by the pike to eat the smaller fish. That's learned helplessness.

Trained elephants grow to have enormous size and strength, yet they are easily kept in place by a relatively small chain and a stake in the ground. That is because, when they are young and small, they are tethered to an enormous chain and stake until they learn that they are powerless to overcome its hold. As the elephant grows to full size, it is no longer necessary to have a large chain to hold them. Almost any chain will do. I could give numerous other examples of learned helplessness, but these two should suffice. For human beings, we don't even need real chains. The only chains necessary are imaginary.

Typically, when we humans compare ourselves to our animal friends, we take great pride in our superior ability to use our intellectual gifts. Far too many individuals are left chained to the stake of learned helplessness. Just like the elephant, we are held captive by our false, self-limiting beliefs.

Almost all helplessness is nothing more than a mental cage we put ourselves in. However, once in place, helplessness is not imagined. It becomes real. Henry Ford's old adage, "If you think you can or you think you can't, you are right," is absolutely true for both points of view. The saddest part of this knowledge is that is it usually extremely difficult to change the minds of those who endlessly quote reasons or excuses regarding why their case is special or different, and therefore, exempt from the idea that they have the power to help themselves.

The truth of the matter is that the road to hell is frequently not paved with good intentions. It is paved with ignorance and apathy along the path of least resistance.

Some things are impossible. I can't jump over a twenty-story building. But the undeniable fact that some things are impossible should never stop me from testing and pushing the limits of what I can do. There are far fewer limits to things that are possible than most people imagine—once our belief and enthusiasm encourages us to try.

If you don't believe that is true, try explaining your opinion to the paraplegic mountain climber who recently climbed Half Dome, Yosemite's 5,000-foot vertical cliff, all by himself.

Read the story of Roger Bannister, the first man in history to break the impossible four-minute mile. This is now the *minimum expectation* of every world-class runner who runs in one-mile competitions.

Ask the team of doctors who transplanted the first human heart, or ask the first man to walk on the moon what is and is not possible.

About once a week, I find a story in the news about ordinary people who have transformed their lives because of necessity or desire. If you will just look for them, you will find them as well.

Here is one such story:

It has been a long time since an 82 mm mortar round in Vietnam transformed Bob Wieland's six-foot, 205-pound body to its current size, without legs, to less than three feet tall and 87 pounds. Bob says, "It almost ruined my day."

Although missing both legs and pronounced dead at the field hospital, Bob became a world record holder in the bench press and Ironman Triathlon. He even did a stint as a strength training coach for the Green Bay Packers football team. He is also a college graduate, author, motivational speaker and true success story in every sense of the word.

Helen Keller became deaf, blind, and unable to speak shortly after her birth. If you ever doubt the human capacity to achieve the seemingly impossible, read her story. Her entire life is a shining example of the fact that no one is ever defeated until they themselves accept their own defeat as reality.

Although each of us is given a start in life with a different set of tools and skills, no one has a valid excuse for not trying. Am I being too hard on underachievers? I think not.

In 2000, New Hampshire State Representative Peter Leonard stood in front of the central podium of the largest legislative body in the United States (and most other places in the world). He was greeted by more than 400 representatives, who stood and applauded his courage, as he said, "Thank you for your tolerance and support. I am now reading at the third grade level and I will continue to do better."

Peter is one spiritually tough cookie. Life has always been tough for him. He has always struggled with, what most consider simple educational goals and he does not have a financially supportive family. He also did not win his election the easy way. In fact, it took him seven election attempts before he succeeded. His speeches are not in the eloquent and flowing style of other politicians, but there is no one who questions his intense devotion to the idea of genuinely serving the needs of his community of loyal voters. He has kept his legislative efforts focused on matters affecting education and the rights of the handicapped. He is learning disabled, *but he is not someone suffering from learned helplessness.*

Shortly after this speech, Peter signed a contract for the screen rights to his life's story with the writer and producer of the highly successful movie, *Flipper.* All of his success occurred primarily because he has a quality most losers lack: positive self-esteem.

Oprah Winfrey was born to an unwed, thirteen-year-old mother. Oprah gave birth to her own child as an unwed, thirteen-year-old child herself. What chance would you have given her of creating a successful and happy life at that time?

PERCEPTION

One morning, over thirty years ago, I woke up with an idea running through my mind. I found a piece of paper and jotted it down. I wanted to save the thought so I could look back upon it as I grew older to see if the simplicity of it still made good sense later in life. I carried it in my wallet until it became worn and almost unreadable. I later preserved it for posterity with a layer of Scotch tape. I have always believed that good ideas are worth saving. It has now stood my personal test of time. Throughout the years, it frequently helped me maintain my balance and comparative perspective in difficult times. Perhaps it will do the same for you.

We live in a world that is but a speck in the universe, smaller than a grain of sand on all of the beaches of the world; where time has no beginning and no end; where distance is greater that infinity. Each person has no more than a few years to spend here, so why waste time worrying about things like a hole in your sock?

This quote is not intended to make light of holes in our socks or more disturbing difficulties we all face on our separate but shared journey through life. It is merely to help put circumstances that are frequently given too much importance in our lives into their proper perspective. It is this kind of perspective that gives each of us the opportunity to step back from the difficulties of the moment and see their true significance in the larger scheme of things. In that regard, I always like to keep in mind the following quote, as it is applied to self-esteem:

There are only two rules in life regarding self-esteem:
Rule #1: Don't sweat the small stuff.
Rule #2: It's all small stuff.

SOLUTIONS

The good part about learned helplessness and poor self-esteem is that they are both solvable with small, successive steps that can easily change how we feel about ourselves. This is true even for those of us who live our lives with extreme cases of undesirable physical appearance or intellectual limitations.

Poor self-esteem and learned helplessness are about comparative failures, such as: failure to achieve; failure to be; failure to win; failure to know; and failure in almost anything and everything you perceive important. In reality, failure is nothing more or less than the sum of the attitudes and beliefs you choose to adopt.

Thomas Edison was once asked by a reporter how he felt about having done over 10,000 experiments, all of which failed. He responded by saying, "I did not fail. I simply learned 10,000 ways not to invent a light bulb. I learned a great deal about what did not work."

Like Thomas Edison, each of us will fail at many things in life. A few will be big, and many will be small. The secret to high self-esteem and success is to not accept the criticism of others or any failed effort as a personal defeat, but rather as a momentary setback or a lesson learned on your journey to higher ground and a better life. Don't blow the importance of any failure out of proportion. Every failure is valuable in and of itself. Accept it for what it is: a valuable insight to be stored in the experience file, giving you another building block to step upon and to grow from. After storing it in your mental file, let it go and move on. You have far more productive and fun things to do on the road to happiness than to cry in your beer.

High self-esteem is necessary in order to have greater success. As previously stated, we only receive those things we believe we deserve. Before you can attain greater success, you must first feel worthy to receive and accept success. Unless you find ways to feel that you deserve more than you have, you cannot achieve your goal for a better life. You must first earn a deeper self-respect for yourself. That will take work, but it will not be nearly as difficult as you might imagine.

You must first temporarily suspend your prior attitudes and judgments about what your abilities are and are not. Next, give yourself permission to try something new.

With just a few short-term goals written down and reviewed on a regular basis, you will soon be amazed at the incredible difference a little change can make.

THINK BIG, START SMALL.

It's a cinch by the inch, hard by the yard.

As previously mentioned, it is very important to start with just one or two goals and a few small steps for each goal that you can put to work immediately. With these small actions, you can build upon each and every small success. In time, these small successes become big successes, and as you get better at this daily exercise, you can begin adding to the number of goals you want to take action on each day. After a relatively short time, you will find this to be as easy and natural as breathing.

Breaking down big goals and problems into smaller parts is a winning technique that all successful people use. Approaching big problems with this mindset lets you stay in control. Otherwise, you may find yourself getting bogged down on what appears to be a single, insurmountable problem. The power of this concept should never be underestimated!

Shortly after the end of World War II, Edward Demming was sent to Japan by the United States government to help the Japanese people rebuild their shattered economy. For quite a few years following the war, the Japanese were known worldwide as the manufacturers of poor quality, cheap merchandise. As a child, I remember most Japanese products being held together by small metal tabs positioned around the edges of individual parts. The tabs were bent over at the time of assembly to hold the parts together. Needless to say, this method was rather ineffective, and the tabs had a very bad habit of breaking off. Anything that was made bearing the label "Made in Japan" in the 1950's was automatically synonymous with cheap and unreliable.

One of the techniques Demming introduced to Japanese manufacturers was *Kazen. Kazen* is the process of small, but never-ending, improvements in everything one does. As a result of the *Kazen* philosophy, each employee is encouraged to find small ways to improve each part of every product in any way possible, no matter how small the improvement. Each change was almost insignificant at the time it was implemented. However, over time, Japan became a world manufacturing super power, and the Japan we know today produces many products that set the standard for quality throughout the world. As a result of *Kazen*, they also now own a disproportionately large share of the worldwide market for manufactured goods.

The message here is simple: Never underestimate the power of small, constant improvements. What worked for them will also work for you.

Since every positive activity you engage in needs a good dose of positive reinforcement to keep you motivated, every effort you make should be rewarded with some sort of recognition. This small-step method allows you to repeatedly reward yourself with the very gratifying pleasure associated with solving small problems rather than waiting for a final, big, end result before holding your celebration. As you may recall, *it is the journey, not the destination* that we strive to enjoy more fully. This small-step methodology fits this purpose perfectly.

ACTION STEP #1 - MAKE A LIST OF YOUR ASSETS

I am not talking about money or material things. I am talking about your unique, personal assets. It does not matter what others do or achieve compared. What matters is what you do with the things that are your own unique assets. You know the ones I am talking about—the assets fate and experience hands us. Each of us is dealt a unique hand of cards in life. Although the cards may all look the same on the top side, the numbers and faces on the player's side contain all kinds of jokers and wild cards that can be played in multiple ways. Your job is to find the best ways to play your life's cards.

No two human beings are identical. That is even true of identical twins. They may look identical, but the combined biological and emotional properties of each are different and unique. You are a totally unique individual. *There is no one like you. There never has been, and there never will be.* The fact that we somehow learn to live a life with feelings based on constant comparative analysis does not alter this fact.

YOUR UNIQUE ASSETS

Can you sing? Are you a good reader? Do you have a natural talent for loving and helping people? Do you speak more than one language? Are you good with your hands? Are you good with mechanical things? Do you have a good memory? Do you like to learn new things? Are you adventurous by nature? Do you enjoy cooking? Are you tall? Are you short? Do you have great hair? Are you very strong? Are you good with children? Do you laugh a lot? Can you find pleasure and beauty in simple things? Do you have good computer skills? Can you program your television and audio equipment without help?

You get the idea. Now it is your turn. Stop reading and get a piece of paper and a pencil right now. **Before reading further, write down what you feel are your top twenty unique personal assets and best skills.**

Take your time. Really think about it. After you have completed this list, set it aside for later review. Before you go to sleep tonight, take this list to the bedroom with you, review it once again, and leave it where you can easily find it again in the morning. That's it. That's all you have to do.

In the morning, pick up the list and add anything else that comes to mind. You will be surprised at the number of things you can add to your list. You can repeat this exercise each evening and morning, and revise this list as often as you would like. Once you feel comfortable that you have listed all your unique assets, put this list on your refrigerator or bathroom mirror so you are reminded of it every day.

Without any other special effort, you will soon find that you better understand and appreciate how special you are and how nice it is to possess each one of your unique assets. Best of all, every one of your unique assets is a valuable tool to be used in the future to help you succeed in reaching the larger goals you list for yourself later on in this book.

Learn to mind your mind, because it controls your future.

All too frequently, we get caught up in the self-defeating game of comparing ourselves to movie stars, intellectual giants, or perhaps the person we think is so great who goes to our school or lives down the street. This kind of self-analysis is a loser's game. *You are not a loser, so kick the habit._*

BEST EFFORTS

Each small step closer to the achievement of a worthwhile goal should be celebrated as a personal victory, because that is what it is. Adopt the habit of accepting the results of every one of your best efforts as a success. No matter where you start, or how far you go, it will always be the continuous progression of these small victories that will be the source of all of your self-confidence and self-esteem.

Even if you think you are not doing well in your struggle to become a better you, others will think highly of you if they see that you are always giving your best effort. Almost everyone I have ever met has expressed far greater admiration and respect for individuals of limited resources who give a 100% effort to life than they do to someone who manages to slide through life with little effort because of innate intelligence, unearned wealth, "connections," or any other method not connected to honest effort.

The admiration and appreciation shown for every person competing in the Special Olympics is a shining example of this natural reaction to hard work and best efforts. If you are always willing to give your best effort at your job, your school, your social organization, or in any other activity, *you will be noticed and appreciated beyond your own personal awareness.* As a result, unexpected opportunities will come your way. This almost always happens to those who conduct their lives with their best effort. When you change, the world automatically changes around you. The unique power of persistence within the *Kazen* method often surpasses the results of natural talent or genius alone.

THE FAILURE GAP

It is just normal human behavior to assume that the gap between success and failure is probably a huge one. That is almost always an incorrect assumption. When we fail, we often think that it just isn't possible to reach our goals without some stroke of good luck or super human effort. More often than not, the truth of the matter is that we just need to increase and maintain our skills or efforts by just a small percentage above our current level. In reality, the gap is seldom very wide. If you only read one more book per month, or make one more sales call each week, or stay one hour later at work each day, or do any of the other things you could be doing with the time you are now probably wasting sitting in front of the TV, you will be amazed at how quickly that success gap closes. Increase your effort and focus by a very small percentage; it truly is cinch by the inch.

ELIMINATE SELF-SABOTAGING IDEAS, ACTIONS AND RELATIONSHIPS

Forgive yourself for past mistakes. Forgive others for their thoughtlessness and ignorance. You are now set on a new path. You don't want anchors from the past to slow you down. You need your full attention focused on the future and the things you are about to do to create a newer, better you. Take a deep breath. Hold it for a moment, and then let it go. Do the same with your past failures, angers, and regrets. Take a deep breath, exhale, and then let them go. They are the enemies of progress and a roadblock on the journey to becoming a new and better you. The new person you are about to become will feel far more joy if you stop dragging self-sabotaging memories behind you for the rest of your life.

Don't let others stop you because they will feel smaller or less successful as your success grows. Give them the opportunity to learn, grow, and change with you if they wish, but do not be held back from becoming a better person because others feel threatened by your progress. When you grow, it is not possible for everybody else to grow at the same rate as you. Personal growth is an individual choice, and each individual must find his or her own comfort level.

When you choose to change, you will almost inevitably get some sort of negative expressions of doubt from at least one person you know. Don't argue with them. Thank them for their opinions, and then respectfully ask them to reserve judgment until you have the opportunity to try out your new wings of freedom from old, limiting ideas and beliefs. Never forget that it is extremely difficult to learn to soar like an eagle if you allow your thinking to be guided by a flock of turkeys.

Once you quit trying to explain and understand what you believe and what your limits are, and instead continually focus your thoughts upon what your possibilities are each and every day, you will soon discover that the sky's the limit.

NEVER STOP GROWING

The truly educated never graduate.

Once you reach each goal, immediately sit down and decide what else you would like to accomplish or become. Without new worthwhile goals, you will once again begin to stagnate, and happiness will begin to dissipate into thin air. A life without purpose is one you will soon find to be less satisfactory than it could be.

RECOMMENDED READING;

The Psychology of Self-Esteem, by Nathaniel Branden

I'm OK - You're OK, by Thomas A Harris, M.D.

Born To Win, by Muriel James and Dorothy Jongward

A Bipolar Life: 50 Years of Battling Manic-Depressive Illness Did Not Stop Me From Building a 60 Million Dollar Business,
by Steve Millard

Chapter 4

The Ladder of Success

Before you climb the ladder of success, first check to see that it is leaning against the right building.

As you should be able to tell by now, my definition of success is about lot more than just money. Let me share it with you:

To live your life in your own way... To reach the goals you have set for yourself... To be the you that you want to be... To be able to reach for the stars without fear... To never lose hope. To find wisdom and humor in every day. That is success.

People are often confused by the fact that my mission as a Certified Financial Planner is not just about teaching people to become more financially successful. It is true that people come to me to learn about better wealth accumulation and preservation techniques, and I don't deny my interest in, or apologize for, that aspect of my profession. I'm very happy I am able to teach them ideas that help in their quest for financial independence. But financial independence is just one item on a long list of worthwhile things to accomplish.

I love the romantic idea of living on love. But, in the real world, money is usually the tool of choice to get the results we need and want for many aspects of our lives. Financial security is extremely important for the peace of mind each of us seeks as we leave adolescence and accept the responsibility of caring for ourselves and the others we love. Therefore, for most people, having financial goals is not inconsistent with attaining greater control and happiness.

Although financial independence can be of great comfort, no one should ever confuse money alone with success. There is only one success and that occurs in your mind. It is immediately translated and monitored each second by how you feel: Are you satisfied or dissatisfied?

Money, like a lot of other material things, can give you security and pleasure, it is true. But if you knew you had only one week to live, you certainly wouldn't choose to spend your final days counting your money over and over again. If you hadn't realize it before, you would discover that the way you have lived your life, which is the legacy you are about to leave the people you care most about, is what matters most.

I don't want to discourage you from setting financial goals. I believe they are, indeed, very important for more than just the obvious reasons. But I would discourage you from making them the centerpiece of your quest for success. A life looked back upon without regret is usually the result of having lived life with goals and values that provide adequate balance in many aspects of life; not just one.

Before you set in motion any plan of action to achieve your financial and material goals, I'd strongly suggest you set down in writing the principles by which you intend to live.

If you were raised as a Christian, you might want to start with the list handed down by Moses. In fact, every religion I have studied has a good list in one form or another. If you don't feel comfortable with a list originating from religious scriptures, you might want to consider starting with a model similar to the one written down long ago by Benjamin Franklin.

FRANKLIN'S THIRTEEN GOALS

Temperance: Eat not to dullness. Drink to elevation.

Silence: Speak not but what may benefit others or yourself. Avoid trifling conversations.

Order: Let all your things have their places. Let each part of your business have its time.

Resolution: Resolve to perform what you ought. Perform without fail what you resolve.

Frugality: Make no expense but to do good to others or yourself; i.e. waste nothing.

Industry: Lose no time. Be always employed in something useful. Cut off unnecessary actions.

Sincerity: Use no hurtful deceit.

Justice: Wrong none by doing injuries or omitting the benefits that are your duty.

Moderation: Avoid extremes. Forebear resenting injuries so much as you think they deserve.

Cleanliness: Tolerate no uncleanness in body, clothes, or habitation.

Tranquility: Be not disturbed by trifles, or at accidents common or unavoidable.

Chastity: Rarely use venery but for health or offspring; never to dullness, weakness, or the injury of your own or another's peace or reputation.

Humility: Imitate Jesus and Socrates.

Don't beat yourself up if you don't achieve all of the high values and goals you set for yourself. Even Ben Franklin noted in his biography that he failed to achieve one of his goals: humility. Being a truthful man, he admitted that every time he became humble, he felt compelled to brag about it.

If you intend to capture happiness and financial independence, it is absolutely essential that your goals be aligned with an excellent value system before you start. Remember this: No matter how good it looks on the outside, a bad core always rots the whole apple in time.

All of the above may have left you with the impression that you may have to sacrifice your most wished for financial goals in order to live by the higher principles alluded to. That need not be the case at all. The idea that wealthy people cannot be virtuous or happy is a myth handed down by those who have little knowledge of wealthy people, and are unaware of the wonderful gifts that have been shared with humanity by those who have achieved great financial success.

F. Scott Fitzgerald once wrote, "The rich are different from you and me," to which fellow novelist, Ernest Hemingway, replied, "Yes, they have more money."

People with wealth who are good at heart tend to stay that way. Even people who may not have been very generous with their wealth in the past frequently become astonishingly generous when they see their life drawing to a close. Andrew Carnegie's gift of establishing the first worldwide free public library system is a great example of such generosity. He built over 3,000 free public libraries in the United States alone, and many more around the world. He also left a large amount of assets in trust so that the funds would be able to provide for the completion of many worthwhile social goals as far into the future as the imagination could see.

NEVER AIM FOR LOW RESULTS

> *There are only two ways to live your life. One is as if everything is a miracle, and the other is as if nothing is.*
> —Albert Einstein

> *Never aim for low results, or you will achieve them.*

As long as you are going to set a few goals for yourself, there is no point in aiming for small results. Setting low goals is a sure sign of low self-esteem. If you don't have at least a few grand goals in life, one of the goals you might want to consider is the goal of significantly raising your self-esteem to the level of someone you know who knows how to succeed, even in difficult situations.

While aiming for the stars is a fine place to shoot for when visualizing long-term goals, you need to be more realistic when setting goals with very short time limits. Setting goals such as, "I want to be a millionaire by the end of the year," when you only have $36 in the bank and no unique skill to speak of just sets yourself up to fail. It is far better to aim for short-term goals that are only 10% or 20% above what you think is reasonable in the first few months.

Notice that I didn't say *aim for what you think is reasonable*. In order to fly, you must first stretch your wings and make a leap of faith. In doing so you will learn, as all small birds do, that you can do more and accomplish far more than you thought. Sure, you will stumble and make mistakes and have setbacks along the way, but you will also become a better you with each passing day. As you start to see the rate of progress you can make from week to week, then you can more realistically set even higher goals.

Speaking from personal experience, I can tell you that every time I look back at the goals I wrote down in years long since passed, I never cease to be astonished that things I thought were totally unreasonable at the time have come to pass. Let me assure you that these goals were not accomplished because I have some extraordinary gift of mental or physical capacity. It is because I have applied the lessons I now share with you. I offer this personal philosophy for maintaining happiness and sanity while shooting for the stars: If you aim high and only achieve 70% or 80% of what you expect, you will be amazed at the dramatic changes that will take place in your life.

Anyone who sets very high goals should never feel unhappy with a 70% or 80% success rates. Setting very high goals gives you the opportunity to stretch your ability as far as you can. The more you stretch, the more you find you can do. It's immensely satisfying to see how far you can grow, but becoming more than you now are is not about pushing yourself with constant mental anguish. Personal growth is always about competing against your own potential. When you do, you are always a winner, even when things don't go your way.

Set goals higher than what you believe you can achieve. You want to give yourself the chance to test your limits, not your limitations. I have asked you this question once before, but it is such a good question that it bears repeating: What goals would you set for yourself if you knew you could not fail?

Not long ago, folks got ink on their hands from changing typewriter ribbons. People actually cranked cars by hand to get them started. If you are over fifty, you no doubt remember *watching radio*, (yes, watching) not television, as a child. Not that long ago, ice was still being cut from lakes in the winter for delivery by horses in the summer. Those who flew wore leather helmets and sat in open cockpits. Just a few years ago, cell phones weighed ten pounds and were carried in a bag. No more than thirty years ago, computers typically filled a room, and the Internet didn't even exist.

Everything you see around you is the completion of a goal that was once nothing more than an idea in someone's mind—the mind of someone who dared to dream and believe that they could do more and become more than what they were. They number in the tens of millions. Their message to you is this: If I can achieve seemingly impossible goals, you can too. You don't have to invent the Internet to be happy. But you do need to have some worthwhile goals in your life.

Each exercise of positive action toward your goal is a victory in and of itself. It is a victory over old habits and inaction. Rest assured that, in time, you will reach the goals you set for yourself. Perhaps not fully in the way you expected, but they will still be victories beyond your wildest dreams.

As soon as you feel you have reached any particular goal, it is important that you immediately set another goal to take its place so you do not lose your momentum. Remember that a life without goals is like a ship without a rudder. In time, you will find this can really get to be fun, especially when you accomplish things others think you can't.

Don't depend on achieving goals alone to make you happy. Learn to enjoy the progress you make rather than focusing exclusively on the end result. Remember that your real goal is to live a happier life every day, not in the future.

Make sure that you choose a few goals to help you make a difference, and not just a living. These goals add immense meaning to your life, not just your financial success. Ultimately, you may find that these *making difference goals* have been the best goals of all.

Imagine that you were awakened by a dream last night. In this dream, you were presented with a box containing a note with the reason for your life printed on it. What did the note say? What would you like it to say? Is the answer associated with any of the goals you have written down? If it is not, you had better rethink your goals.

What is your ultimate destiny? What do you want your life to be? If your life is not now everything you would like it to be, when do you think would be the best time to start making some changes?

This is no time to start kidding yourself. There is no better time than right now. Make a decision right now to no longer make excuses for not starting immediately on the journey to your most important goals.

Write down two things you are going to do, before the end of the day, today, that will make a positive change in your life. Now do them. I promise; you are going to enjoy this.

Chapter 5

Vision

THE POWER OF VISUALIZATION

Imagine, if you will, that your life is like a horizontal line. Take out a sheet of paper and draw a straight line across the sheet, from left to right. On the extreme right-hand end of the line, write down the words, "age 0." On the left end of the line, write the words, "age 100." Between 0 and 100, divide the line into five-year, numbered increments. Now circle the number nearest your current age. Now circle the age of your anticipated retirement age , and also your life expectancy based upon your family history.

What percentage of your life expectancy is already gone? If you had some of the prior years back to do over again, how would you use the years that you now see as wasted? It is never too late to change past habits. Your time is more limited than you think. For each year that passes, you have less and less time to accomplish any long-term goals. Without cementing a few important goals in your mind right now, you are cheating yourself out of year after year of building a better life.

Cherish your vision and your dreams as they are the children of your soul; the blueprints of your ultimate achievements.

—Napoleon Hill

I first read about the power of visualization in the book *Psycho-Cybernetics*, by Dr. Maxwell Maltz, almost thirty years ago. The theme of his book is that people can only change when they change their current view of themselves to the vision of who they would like to become. I found this to be true. This is a great book, and remains on my must read list for people who want an in-depth look at the psychology of visualization. However, one of the book's contentions is that by practicing visualization of the outcome you want for a minimum of twenty-one days, you will change the habits that control your life. Although this is helpful, I personally found that I needed more than this idea alone in order to make any meaningful change in the direction of my life. More recent research indicates that the average time needed to permanently change a habit is actually 66 days. Obviously, individual results can vary a great deal.

Since that time, I have practiced several different visualization techniques. Some worked better than others, but I really never found any that had a magic formula for quick success. Having said that, however, did not and does not diminish in the least the incredible importance of visualization as part of any successful venture. While I found no quick success, I did find a sure-fire method for long-term visualization success. That technique is the same 3x5 index card system briefly mentioned in Chapter Two.

The reason this system works, and others do not, is because of two basic differences. First and foremost, by writing down your vision of the future in detail on 3X5 cards, those future goals remain very consistent on a day-to-day basis. The second reason is because the card reminders are so convenient and easy to use that I am able to carry they around, and actually review them several times each day, until they were firmly fixed in my mind. They can be stored in a shirt pocket, a briefcase, a lunch bucket, a wallet, or a purse with ease. They don't take up much room. Those simple facts make all the difference in the world.

You will become what you think about most.

Even if you do not take the time to go through the deep visualization process we talked about in the previous chapter, each time you review one of your 3x5 cards, you reinforce that goal on a regular basis. If, in the beginning, you have a clear picture in your mind of what you want, it won't be hard to visualize something very close to that picture again and again, with the constant reminder provided by the cards.

If, instead of 3X5 cards, you decide you just want to keep your goals written on writing tablets or some electronic device, you're most likely going to find these writing pads in the not-so-distant future on a shelf somewhere, covered with dust, and long since forgotten or forgotten within computer files.. To carry out Dr. Maltz's idea of visualization for at least twenty-one days or longer, you will need the help of these little 3x5 cards. Trust me on this.

The cards have another benefit so often overlooked. Taking the time to summarize your goal on a 3x5 card forces you to state the goal in clear and simple terms. There isn't a lot of room on each card, so your thinking must be concise. Additionally, the very act of writing sends another clear message to your sub-conscious mind telling it that you are serious about this goal

LASTING CHANGE REQUIRES STRUCTURE

If you think you can create lasting change without structure, think again. In the pursuit of change, your own habits will be your greatest foe. Without constant visual reminders the 3x5 cards prompt, you don't stand a prayer of a chance for change. If you have no well-defined vision and a structured action plan for getting there, you are heading toward certain failure. The person who controls his or her mind controls their destiny. Without control, the mind loses its effectiveness. To control your destiny, you must act now, act small, and act repeatedly. The 3x5 card system lets you do that with ease.

For example, if you find you are having trouble visualizing your future for any of your listed goals, that is a pretty good indication that you are a bit out of practice in imagining and visualizing part of your life. Not to worry. You have a great imagination. Your visualization technique is not in doubt, either. Both of these attributes are as natural to each of us as breathing. Think back to when you were seven or eight years old. You know, that time in your life before the people in your life kept telling you not to be a free spirit; a time before you allowed yourself to limit your imagination and expectations.

If you are a man, you probably saw yourself as a cowboy, a fireman, or a tractor operator—and a darn good one at that. You got out your six-shooter, your fireman's hat, or your toy tractors and had no trouble playing each role with total belief. You could do this even if there was no one else to play with.

In my generation, if you are a girl, think back to all the times you played with your dolls. You were most likely mother, nurse, and teacher to a whole generation of make-believe children. You were the best. You never thought twice about becoming absorbed into those roles and having a wonderful time living your dreams.

If you still doubt your ability to visualize well today, as an adult, think back to your last really good or weird dream.

If you are serious about reaching your most important goals, the most effective kind of visualization you can practice is the same kind you practiced when you were a child. The biggest obstacle between what you are, what you have today, what you want to become, and what you want to have in the future is between your ears.

The roles you are going to play in the future begin and end in your mind. Even if you still want to be a cowboy or an actress today, you can do it. Only you stand in the way. You can be anything you want if you first create the role in your mind.

VISIONEERING

In 1914, when Tom Watson was forty, he joined a company that made products like meat slicers and punch card machines. Ten years later, he became the president of the company, and renamed it International Business Machine to better fit his goal of where he wanted to go. You may better recognize this once small company as Big Blue or IBM. Men like Watson do not act on ideas alone. They act on vision. The ideas they need to fulfill their vision almost always come later.

You are the CEO of your life, and without imagination, (another word for vision) not much positive change will take place. Imagine that you are in charge of running the most important company in the world. It's called, *Your Life, Inc.* You are the only employee, so you have sole authority and control over the direction in which the company is heading. The public (your peers) expects you to produce what they want. But what do you want? What are your own goals?

PLAYING THE PART

As you now look back over the 3x5 cards listing each of the goals you identified in Chapter Two, get into character, as they say in the movies. Imagine that you have already achieved each goal.

Let's say, for example, you wanted to become a college professor. Imagine that it is fall in New England and the leaves have turned to golden yellows and crimson reds. You see a few leaves blowing across your path as your make your way to the lecture hall. Imagine you are now walking into the lecture hall. There is a window in this room, and it is slightly open. You feel the crispness in the clear, cold air. How are you dressed? What are you carrying with you? What does the room look like? What do the students look like? What subject are you going to explore and challenge them with?

If, becoming a college professor is still your goal after answering the questions above, fix that same crisp, clear vision in your mind. Now attach that vision to a 3x5 card that says, "I am going to become a college professor by (fill in the date)." If you really want this goal, and you are willing to take some form of positive action every time you view this card, you will be a college professor. No one can stop you except you! The clearer the image you create for each goal, the greater your success will be.

Your subconscious mind cannot tell the difference between the image you make up and the real world in which you are now living. If you repeatedly give your mind a clear picture of what you want, your subconscious mind will do an incredible job of steering you straight to the doorstep of that goal.

FAKE IT 'TIL YOU MAKE IT

Imagination is more important than fact
—Albert Einstein

If you are serious about expanding your capabilities and changing who you are, you need to act differently today.
Fake it 'til you make it is a bit harsh as a description for the kind of role-playing you need to do, but it's not far off track. If you intend to change, it is an excellent exercise to get into your new

role in every way you can. You will be amazed by the difference just one small thing, like a new suit of clothes, can make in your attitude and actions. If you see yourself as financially successful, buy a nice piece of tasteful jewelry or a beautiful silk tie to go with the new outfit.

This role-playing is far more effective than most people realize. If you were to ask a superstar in any profession, you would almost certainly find that they use role-playing and mental rehearsals. They mentally go over the exact performance they expect to give in their mind until they see themselves, and the success they are looking for, clearly etched in their mind. When they cannot practice the real thing, mental rehearsal is a powerful substitute. They do this over and over again, to perfection. In most cases, this mental practice is better than the real thing. That's because you will never fail in your mind unless you choose to do so. It's simple and requires no equipment other than your mind. Therefore, you can do it any place and any time you find convenient. The amazing thing is that these imaginary instructions to your brain work fabulously. Russian and East German Olympic trainers studied and used these methods for more than forty years in order to maximize the performances of their athletes.

To stimulate ideas, and to help with the vision you want to fix into your mind, let me suggest a source you may not otherwise think about. If your new destination includes a group that has a specialty publication (I can't think of any that don't these days), get a subscription and read every issue, cover to cover.

Now, to further clarify your vision, introduce yourself to someone who does what you want to do or become, and who has your respect and the respect of the community you plan to live within in the future. Arrange to meet them. Tell them you are serious about making this change in your life, and you would appreciate the opportunity to get their point of view. Ask them what kind of questions you should be asking, and who else they might suggest who may have helpful insights about your chosen goal. Offer to buy them a great lunch at their favorite restaurant. It may well be is the best business expense you will ever pay for. The ideas and visions that this person can set in motion for you will be invaluable.

Don't be bashful about this. You will find that even very important and busy people are flattered by such a request, and are pleased to be able to help. Asking for help is not a sin. It is a blessing that gives others the opportunity to contribute to your success. It gives them the opportunity to feel good about themselves. It is not your place in life to deny them that opportunity.

RECOMMENDED READING;

Psycho-Cybernetics, by Dr. Maxwell Maltz

Chapter 6

Belief

THE POWER TO CREATE OR DESTROY

What is the force in our lives that determines what we become or fail to become? It is our beliefs.

Whatever the mind can conceive and believe it can achieve.
—Napoleon Hill

There is a treasure stored between your ears. By learning to clarify and focus your thoughts, you have the ability to unearth whatever treasure you want for yourself. First you must believe you can. All personal breakthroughs start with a change in beliefs. Your beliefs determine your potential for success by either turning off or turning on the flow of new ideas. Have you set negative or positive beliefs and expectations in your life as your guideposts along life's path?

Belief is such a powerful force, that an ice cube can cause a blister to form on the skin of hypnotized subjects who are touched by ice after they are told that it is something very hot. If you had that level of belief in your ability to succeed, it would change your life. Success is not based upon luck or accident; it is the result of your beliefs. One person with passion and a strongly held belief has more impact on the future than a thousand people who have only interest.

Whether you think you can or think you can't, you are right.
—Henry Ford

It is our beliefs that drive our entire behavior. Belief is what determines what we try and how long we are willing to persist in any effort involving an uncertain outcome.

Beliefs come in three different strength levels. The weakest is opinion, which we may or may not easily decide to change.

The next level of belief is cultural belief. These beliefs are based upon our culture's general value system. They are also influenced by where we grew up, the political beliefs of our parents, the religious teachings we have absorbed, racial and ethnic heritage, gender, age, our peers, and numerous other factors that our social background has introduced us to. These beliefs are based upon accepting the individual's environmental and cultural heritage, and are usually acquired without much critical examination or worldly perspective.

The third level of belief is conviction. These are beliefs so deep in the marrow of our bones that they are almost unshakable. Unfortunately, these beliefs are frequently harmful, rather than helpful, to your goal of greater happiness. They are powered over time by enthusiasm and continual reinforcement. These beliefs are a set of theories we develop, and by which we run our lives.

Sometimes these beliefs are so strong they can virtually change us physically. That is why researchers use double-blind drug tests to sort out the placebo effect, which always occurs in a certain percentage of test patients who have received nothing but sugar pills. Simply because they believe they received a newly developed solution to their medical complaint, they totally or partially cure themselves, simply because they believe that new test drugs will do what researchers suggest may occur. When you are totally convinced about a thing in your mind, the results are amazing.

One of the greatest obstacles on the road to the future you desire is changing ineffective, harmful, or misguided beliefs that are deeply ingrained in the complex workings of your mind.

Over time, we all accumulate lots of general beliefs without giving them much thought. Many of these beliefs are induced by the media. If there is any doubt in your mind regarding this, you may find the statistical information that follows a thought-provoking look at media-induced beliefs versus actual statistical facts.

THE ODDS ARE:

1 in 4	You will die prior to age 65
1 in 25	You will die in an automobile accident
1 in 1000	You will undergo an IRS audit this year
1 in 6,000	Your child will suffer a high chair injury
1 in 25,000	You will develop a brain tumor
1 in 40,000	You will die in a fire this year
1 in 300,000	You will be hit by a major league baseball
1 in 46,000,000	You will die in an U.S. airplane crash

Ask yourself this question: Do you feel safer when you get into your car to drive to the airport, or when your plane roars down the runway on takeoff? Why is it flying worries us more? How many of our beliefs are shaped by the media?

According to a one *Boston Globe* article, airlines in the U,S, carried 600 million passengers on 9,500,000 different flights in 1997. Only two passengers died in accidents that year. You probably won't remember that statistic, but you will always remember at least one past, highly publicized, airline disaster that repeatedly discussed on the evening news. Captain Sully's forced landing on the Hudson River on January 15, 2009 is one example. That amazing landing saved 155 passengers from otherwise near certain death. It also helped keep airline accidental death rates statistics to almost zero in every year since. Yet millions of people are still more fearful when flying than they are driving their car, where 40,000 people die every year. This response is called a *conditioned reflex.*

Pavlov understood these automatic responses very well. He simply rang a bell and gave each dog food. After their training period ended, the dogs salivated at the sound of each bell, even though no food was given. The dog's conditioned reflex response is not much different from our own. What the media has done is to create expectations and beliefs that cause us to salivate with every food and beverage commercial. We have learned to feel stressed and anxious almost every time we watch the news. This process stimulates us, which helps to sell products and capture market shares for more advertising, but I am not sure that it helps people at all.

Any limitations you now have in your life are determined in large part by limited knowledge and the limitations of your most deeply held beliefs. Many of these beliefs are nothing more than conditioned reflexes. Your beliefs control your expectations about the future, and your expectations determine what you do or don't do.

This is great news. As soon as you begin to apply your own systematic method to reinforce the beliefs necessary for positive change, you control your destiny.

BELIEFS ARE A CHOICE

I know that may sound wrong to you. Many individuals don't believe that what they believe is a choice. That is because they are convinced that their beliefs are simply true facts and not changeable opinions fashioned by others. Many people wrongly believe that what goes on in our mind is based upon facts outside of our control.

In most cases, we have simply learned to accept and believe what we see and experience. It appears that belief is simply the product of observing and experiencing what is clearly true. Some of the time, this is not a bad idea. A lot of the time, however, it leads to poor assumptions and beliefs.

Before Columbus sailed to the New World, a lot of people believed he would sail right off the world's edge. You didn't have to be very smart to see that. Even a fool could stand on any shoreline and see the edge of the world in the distance.

The town of Salem, Massachusetts believed many problems were caused by witches. I'm glad they solved that long before my time. Once upon a time, many westerners believed that *the only good Indian was a dead Indian* (of course, this opinion was not shared by the Westerners who happen to be Indians). Early physicians believed that washing one's hands before proceeding with surgery was unnecessary. They also believed that bleeding people who were ill was helpful to the patient. It got the illness out. I won't bother to go on. By now you understand the need to be careful regarding the beliefs you choose to adopt.

Beliefs are, indeed, a choice. Because this is not well understood, many people don't give much, if any, thought to how the process of belief formation occurs. It seems that one's beliefs are almost automatic, and therefore should be universally understood. Why should you have to question *every fact* you hear? Why not simply accept whatever sounds or appears to be logical? You can, but history frequently demonstrates that is a very bad idea.

Short-cut thinking forms most beliefs. The brain does this in self-defense. Because our sensory systems are bombarded with millions of bits of information day after day, in order to survive, the brain must become a very good split-second decision-maker. Most decisions are based on whatever information can be quickly assimilated, condensed, and simplified enough to be easily recalled in the future.

More often than not, our decisions are based upon short-cut thinking. We don't typically take the time to sort through all of the possibilities life offers to decide what to believe. That's what researchers do—not average people. If we reviewed all available information all of the time, we would not be able to function because of constant information overload. Our sensory system couldn't handle that kind of load. That is why we use short-cut thinking.

In addition to not being able to handle total information absorption all of the time, research shows that our mind is also unable to tolerate unanswered questions. Therefore, we develop theories about what is going on in our lives and how things should be. That is the basis of *right and wrong*, a simplistic theory about how everything ought to be. This concept gets us into a lot of trouble. Nevertheless, each of us is prepared to strongly argue in defense of our beliefs.

Despite this fact, you do have the choice to reserve judgment when you hear new information. You don't need to have a knee-jerk reaction to every challenge to your belief system. This doesn't mean you have to change your beliefs. It just suggests that there is usually more than meets the eye in every situation, and it might be beneficial to keep an open mind.

Let's take the human body as an example of this idea. Reach up and touch your head and answer this question: Is it a solid structure? If you answered, "yes," you might be interested to know that there are a lot of very smart chemists and physicists who tell you that you are dead wrong. In fact, they would gladly bet you that your head is composed of chemical compounds. Those compounds are composed of atoms, which, in turn, are composed of protons, neutrons, and electrons whirling around each other in space. In fact, they will tell you that the distance between the protons, neutrons, and electrons is so far apart that you are actually composed of 99.9% empty space. Your head is not solid at all; it just appears that way because of our inability to see the particles from which it is composed.

I'm sure you won't lose any sleep over this revelation. It is just another interesting fact that doesn't fit easily into a natural, assumption-based belief system.

WHY IS ALL OF THIS STUFF IMPORTANT?

> *You cannot teach a man anything. You can*
> *only help him discover it within himself.*
> —Galileo

It is important because you need to fully accept that you, and no one else, is in charge of your destiny. Your destiny is based upon your beliefs. Your beliefs are the foundation of your personal heaven or hell. You can find good evidence to follow beliefs that support either habits of heaven (positive thinking) or hell (negative thinking). Since you have a choice of which evidence you choose to believe, why choose hell?

Often people have beliefs that cause actions in their lives that are not conducive to helping them to reach the goals they want for themselves. If you can convince yourself to keep an open mind in pursuit of new knowledge, you may well be able to open many new doors of opportunity to a happier life.

Every person has at least a few current beliefs that limit their potential to make quantum leaps forward toward the success we each seek. Before you can make these leaps, however, you must first open your mind and make a leap of faith. You must give these ideas a chance to prove themselves to you. In time, the positive changes that result in your life will automatically change your beliefs.

You can be more successful and happier than you currently believe you can. Unfortunately, however, just acting naturally doesn't allow you to focus your thinking consistently enough of the time on the new ideas necessary to create a high degree of successful change.

In order to succeed, you need a systematic approach that allows you to be consistent in your new way of thinking about things. You need a tried and true method to keep your mind focused on the vision of the future you want for yourself. Positive change requires time and consistent effort; therefore,   to stay on track, you will be well-served by learning to rely on the 3x5 cards containing you new goals.

As time passes, and you experience more and more success with this method, your current self-limiting beliefs and attitudes will change. By following this path, you will learn to form and retain more accurate beliefs regarding your own capacity to achieve the things you once thought were most likely impossible.

Chapter 7

Attitude

The pessimist sees difficulty in every opportunity.
The optimists sees opportunity in every difficulty.

—Sir Winston Churchill

What really shapes our lives is not the events that occur, but the meaning we attach to them. Life is not a problem to be solved; it is an adventure to be explored.

The greatest discovery of any generation is that a human
being can alter his life by altering his attitude.

—William James

We all have many things in common, but one unique factor can make a very big difference. That factor is whether one's attitude is positive or negative. Happiness is far more dependent upon attitudes than circumstances. Our lives are not determined by what life brings, but rather by what attitudes we bring to each day of our life. Positive attitudes cause a chain reaction of positive thoughts, events, and outcomes. A positive attitude is like a magic potion that becomes the catalyst for a continuous, positive change. It is this optimistic attitude that allows positive possibilities to be acted upon whenever they occur.

> *As a man thinketh in his heart, so is he.*
> —Proverbs 23:7

Optimism and positive expectations are like wings that lift you up from where you are to a higher level. That new, higher level enables you to see the possibilities that were once out of sight and just over the horizon.

> *There is nothing in this world more*
> *depressing than a young pessimist.*
> —Mark Twain

If you have negative expectations in your life, those expectations are like an anchor that you drag through life. Negative thoughts hold you back in everything that you attempt to do.

No worthwhile goal was ever achieved by negative thinking!

In 1900, people had an average life expectancy of only forty-nine years. As of 2007, if you live to the age of 65, you could expect to live to age 83.6 years of age, on average.

What about the future? At the University of California at San Francisco, researcher Cynthia Kenyon produced genes in a race of tiny worms that live twice as long as usual because the aging process is slowed down to half the normal speed. Cal Harley, a genetic engineer at Geron, a Menlo Park, California biotech company, is using genetic engineering to restore a cell's telomeres, the protective tips of a chromosome. "They're like the clock of life," Haley says. By inserting a telomere-restoring gene into tissue, Harley has created cells that divide indefinitely. Based upon this research, Harley believes that we could have life spans in the future as long as 200 or 300 years. Given those projections, I'd like to suggest looking for an optimism switch to turn on today. The longer you live, the greater you appreciate living your life as an optimist.

The significant problems we face cannot be solved at the same level of thinking we were at when we created them.

—Albert Einstein

Unless you do something beyond what you already know how to do, you will never grow. If you do not grow, you will not change. If you do not change, your future will be a lot like the life you have now. It is not enough to wish for a better life; you must expect it and work towards making the changes to allow it to happen.

CONTROLLING THE POSITIVE EXPECTATION SWITCH

We are what we think. All that we are arises with

our thoughts.

— Buddha 563-479 B.C.E.

Happiness is directly connected to the expectations and attitudes we choose to adopt and adapt in our lives, rather than a result of the actual circumstances life delivers. If you are happy, it is most likely because the life you are experiencing is either meeting or exceeding your expectations. There are no other reasons. Happiness is not about having what you want—it is about appreciating what you have. Appreciating what you have is about expectations, and if you are not as happy as you would like to be, it is probably because you need an attitude adjustment regarding your expectations. This does not mean that you should have low expectations for fear of being unhappy. Not expecting much is the direct path to low achievement and low self-esteem—not happiness. You usually get what you expect in life, so don't make a habit of expecting very little from yourself.

The path to happiness is found by giving your dreams one hundred percent effort and then taking satisfaction in whatever results you achieve. Your emotional well-being is primarily determined by what you focus your attention upon. Therefore, it is important to learn to focus primarily upon the gains you have made, even if those gains come only in the form of learning a new lesson as the result of a failed effort.

You can achieve happiness even if you set goals you think are beyond what you can achieve during the next year, five years, or ten years, and then fail to fully reach. You will do no harm by being bold and wise enough to ask more of life than you think you may be worth. It is an observable fact that people tend to rise to the expectations that placed upon themselves or others.

When pursuing your dreams, success is not measured by how many times your fall down. Rather, it is measured by how many times you get up.

To be happy, your expectations should be fulfilled if you make significant progress. You need not be disappointed if you do not reach one hundred percent of a goal that was beyond your capability when you started. If you set very difficult goals, you may not reach all those you set for yourself. However, if you give those goals the time and energy they deserve, you will reach at least eighty percent of your full potential. That eighty percent is an extremely good result. That is because, to reach one hundred percent of an extremely difficult goal, you had to sacrifice a big portion of the balance essential to a happy life. If your efforts to achieve one goal cause you to end up damaging other important areas of your life, you need to rethink and revise that goal. While leading an unbalanced life for short periods of time may be okay, eventually, this lopsided approach to life usually leads to trouble.

In order to fulfill your dreams, you will also need some good luck and the help of events you cannot now foresee. Hard work will help to create *good luck* and opportunities that you cannot now imagine. Therefore, set dreams that are 100% or more of your perceived potential, and then be happy reaping the benefits your potential within a balanced lifestyle delivers.

If you give your goals an honest effort, over time you will come to see that your potential is far more than you ever dreamed it could be. You will ultimately discover that there are no limitations except those you impose upon yourself. That knowledge alone is very satisfying.

When setting your dreams into motion, don't set yourself up for failure by setting all-or-nothing goals that mean you fail if you do not achieve one hundred percent of the results you hoped to achieve. Positive expectations are expectations of continual forward movement toward whatever worthwhile goals you set for yourself. As long as you take actions designed to move you closer to your goals, you will always be a success. While you patiently work on each step forward toward your ultimate goal, it is important to be sustained in your daily efforts by an optimistic attitude. Fortunately, optimism is a mental habit one can choose to practice until it becomes habit. Recognizing your small successes goes a long way toward making optimism your constant companion.

GRATITUDE

Although this subject has already been mentioned in Chapter One, it is so important to your persistent happiness it bears repeating again just to be sure that you do not underestimate its power to shape your future.

Gratitude is the key to harmony and happiness. It is the source of great wells of health, strength, and energy. It is the path to wonderful relationships and a river of good ideas those relationships bring. It ought to be first on your list of attitudes to enhance and practice on a daily basis as a mental adjustment for personal and financial prosperity.

It all depends on how we look at things and
not on how they are in themselves.

—Carl Jung

To be truly happy, you must have a genuine attitude of gratitude. Without gratitude for all the wonderfulness existing within your life, you can frequently become dissatisfied without fully appreciating why. The more gratitude you are able to actually feel and express, the more pleasure and happiness fills your life each day. Gratitude is easy to have. As previously mentioned, it simply requires the daily practice of looking for things to be grateful about. Take a 3X5 card right now and write down this question:

What are the three things I are most grateful for today and why?

Now answer that question. If you honestly focus your thoughts on that question each day, you will easily find many things for which to be grateful.

Carry this card with you and review it in the morning, at mid-day, and in the evening each day. If you find yourself grateful for this idea, continue doing it long enough to make it a permanent habit in your life. Once it proves itself to you, you may even decide to teach it to a friend who will also be grateful for the idea..

Gratitude fixes your mind on the positive things of life, and gives you faith in the future. Faith in the future is essential for happiness and success to blossom and grow.

If, after answering the question on your 3X5 card each day, you still are having trouble expressing your gratitude to yourself and others on a daily basis try this: Make a trip to your local hospital. Take a good look at all the cars in the parking lot. Unless the owners of those cars are visiting the hospital to welcome a new baby into the world, I guarantee you there are stories of emotional and physical pain that are connected to almost every car in the lot. It is impossible to imagine how much collective pain is represented by all of those families. Go into the lobby and take a seat. Take a good look at the people who come in and go out. Look closely at their faces. You won't see many who smile or laugh. Imagine, as each person comes into the lobby, that they write down the problem they are visiting about on a small a slip of paper. Next they put it into a big raffle drum, which is sitting on a table next to your chair. Now imagine that you are writing down your own worst problem. Place it into the drum. Now imagine that all the problems listed on the pieces of paper inside that drum are spun around and thoroughly mixed up.

How grateful are you that fate has not chosen you to draw one of their unknown problems out of the drum in exchange for your own?

Even if your life is not perfect, you are probably still better off dealing with the circumstances at hand than taking the risk of exchanging your problems for someone else's.

Did you know that in Zimbabwe, *25% of the entire population is HIV positive?* In the small village of Nthandire, in the poor, landlocked African country of Malawi, there are almost no young men and women at all. The survival rate between age 20 and 40 has been reduced to almost zero because of the AIDS epidemic alone. It is not unusual to see grandparents trying to raise as many as fifteen or more orphaned grandchildren left behind by their several, deceased, sons and daughters.

On the continent of Africa, the estimate of the number of children who die of malaria alone is now between one and three million each year. The exact number is difficult to estimate, because so many poor children have no doctor caring for them at the time of their death who is qualified to determine the exact cause of death. Despite the rampant problem of malaria, millions of African families still lack anti-malarial bed nets to keep them safe at night from infectious mosquitoes. How would you like to swap you problems with any one of these individuals?

The statistics of poverty, disease, and hunger still present in the world are truly staggering and depressing. Suffice it to say, count your blessings, but not your misfortunes.

Don't wait for gratitude and happiness to find you; seek it out. Life is a comparative experience. You have lots of reasons to be both happy and grateful. Think about the happy ones and write them downs.

To have contentment, you must first be a person who finds happiness in everyday events and circumstances. Happiness is experienced moment to moment, and not as an end result. If you are sincere about your pursuit of happiness, even in the face of personal difficulties, you may consider adopting at least a few of the following ideas as daily activities.

Life it too important to be taken seriously.
—Oscar Wilde

Share the jokes you have learned, and the positive ideas you have, with others at home and at work.

There is no scientific proof that life is serious.

Start each day by reading the comic strips in your morning newspaper *before you read the news.* The news will not be good, and you can use something cheerful to dilute it with.

Add a funny calendar to your kitchen counter or desktop to assure that at least one funny thought interrupts your serious thinking each day.

Look for *lucky pennies* on the ground as you walk, and you will find them. Tell yourself during your self-talk that these pennies are lucky, and that you will suddenly find good fortune and pleasure in many of your circumstances. These lucky pennies prompt you to actively look for positive things and good fortune to notice in the world around you. *If you look, you will find them.*

Learn to reward yourself—without guilt—for your personal achievements.

Look around yourself at home and at work or even in public for at least one person to compliment and appreciate each day. Look for the good in people. You will find it is everywhere.

Every day is a gift. That is why it is called the present.

Give your memory a good house-cleaning to remove the dirt and grit of yesterday. Forgive yourself for past failures. Live for the future. Every day is a new beginning of endless, positive possibilities.

Discover the joy of achieving things others believe you cannot do. These things will bring great pleasure to your life.

This list of suggestions could be almost endless, but by now I'm sure you get the idea. Create a written list of your own.

After surviving Hitler's concentration camps of World War II, the famous psychiatrists, Dr. Victor Frankl, said the following in his classic book, *Man's Search for Meaning*;

Everything can be taken from a man but one thing: the last of the human freedoms—to choose one's own way.

Perhaps Dr Frankl's quote explains this bumper sticker:

It's never too late to have a happy childhood.

Life can be altered for the better just by changing the self-talk we have with ourselves on a daily basis. If you want greater happiness, it is your job to find and use techniques that give you a better attitude, which becomes permanent. This is not nearly as elusive or difficult a goal as it may seem. Like all habits, attitudes are changed by the spaced repetition of thoughts, actions, and the positive questions and self-talk we choose to incorporate in our daily discussions with ourselves.

If you write and review your gratitude cards on a daily basis, your attitude and life will be changed forever because you are taking repetitive, positive actions in the direction of your greater happiness goal. This is not a sugar coated denial of problems in your life or the world. It is simply recognition of the fact that you have a choice of what you wish to focus most of your thoughts on. Choosing to focus more of your time on the good rather than the bad is a well established path to greater happiness.

Happiness is not a destination; it is a mode of travel.

WHAT'S YOUR QUESTION?

Our brain is like an acorn with the potential to become a great oak. What we will become is not answered by our genes or written in the stars. Our brain is like a sleeping giant, awaiting only our imagination to bring it to life. We need only a spark from a switch of some sort to turn it on. That switch is none other than the humble question.

The seeds for a bountiful life are a gift implanted deep within our DNA. At the very heart of our nature lies a throbbing impulse that demands freedom. It is the freedom to become something not yet defined. We are biologically designed to transcend the limits of our own biology, to become the creator of that which springs from our imagination. We are designed to continually transcend the limits of whom and what we are. Yet, the breadth of our exploration, and the degree to which we transcend our basic biology, is largely controlled by one thing: the questions we ask and the answers we give ourselves.

Questions are the things that steer the course for our conscious and unconscious mind. What shapes our thinking, and therefore our destiny, are the questions we ask, refuse to ask, or never think of asking. These questions determine whether we are searchers or acceptors of the status quo; whether we are superficial or profound in the use of this gift of life we are given.

To become a questioner is to make a decision to search for wisdom rather than for certainty. Questions, by their very nature, ask us to explore the unknown—to move beyond social habits that tend to inhibit our potential and our spirit.

For most of our lives, we are coached by society regarding how to think about almost everything. As a result, most people live and die within the boundaries and limitations set by those around them.

In the unexamined life, culture asks and answers almost all your questions before you even ask them. When the mind sleeps comfortably beneath the security blanket of cultural answers, it clips the wings of its own potential.

If you wish to recover your birthright of unlimited potential, you must first open the doors of your mind as widely as possible. The key to the door of your mind is none other than a question.

All human progress is always preceded by a question.

The mechanics of success requires change. When we change, everything else in our world also changes. Knowledge alone is not enough to engage the gears of change. Until we decide we want our life to be different, nothing changes. Only four things motivate people to want to change: The first three are boredom, enlightenment, or pain; the fourth is the discovery they can change.

Who you become depends on what questions you ask yourself.

Every human being engages in *self-talk*. *Self-talk* is the internal dialogue we have with ourselves each and every day. Does this look good on me? Is this the kind of person I should be spending time with?

When you begin asking yourself the right questions during daily *self-talk*, you soon discover you can change, and that change is often both quick and dramatic. The questions you ask or fail to ask shape your destiny. If you are *not* looking for answers, you will not find them.

One of the most fascinating and helpful things I have discovered about the mind is that it can and will attempt to answer any question asked of it. That does not mean that the answer will be what you want or expect, or that it will even be correct. If the right questions are asked, you will soon be on the right track to rapidly expanding your potential. It is now just a question of steering your mind in the right direction by providing it with positive questions that elicit positive answers.

If we choose good questions, we have good attitudes and results. If the questions are poor, our attitudes and results are as well. Therefore, if we want to change the quality of our lives, we must first change the quality of the questions we habitually ask ourselves. Do you typically ask, "Why me?" or is your question more like, "How can I benefit from this?"

> *The quality of your life is most often determined by the quality of questions you ask yourself each and every day.*

Imagine someone asking you, "How did you become so smart?" Now, imagine instead, that the question is, "Why are you such a loser?"

What effect would those questions have on your life? How would those questions make you feel? Obviously, the questions we ask others and ourselves have tremendous power. Unfortunately, that is true even if the questions are hurtful or unfair.

The questions you choose to ask can change your life. The only question that remains is what kind of questions will you use in the future—negative questions or positive ones? Unless you are a masochist, the answer should be clear.

People who succeed do not have fewer problems; they just ask better self-talk questions. I will not discuss samples of negative questions you might ask yourself. I don't want to stimulate any negative ideas that may already exist in your life. If you hope to have lasting positive change in your life, it is your job to replace all the negative questions you now have in your life with positive ones. That process is easier than you think. All you need is a good list of questions you can copy onto your 3X5 cards for daily use. What positive questions can you think of that will change your life for the better? Let me get you going in the right direction with a starter kit.

1. If I could only do one thing today to improve the quality of my life, what would that be?
2. If I knew I could not fail, what goals would I set for myself?
3. What opportunity for positive change am I going to take advantage of today?
4. What is wonderful and exciting about my life right now?
5. How can I create more pleasure in my life and the lives of those I meet today?
6. How can this experience help me?
7. What one thing could I do that I am not doing now that would make the best change in my life?
8. What positive things did I learn today?
9. What are my best skills, and how can I better use them?
10. What opportunities does this problem present?
11. What am I most happy about and grateful for?
12. How can I do this better?
13. What new book should I read this week?
14. How can I reorganize my activities to be more effective in reaching my important goals?

Asking good questions creates focus and direction. If the focus of your daily thoughts is upon questions like these, you will create a very fruitful and happy life. Your only challenge is to be sure you always have a handful of cards that ask questions like these, until it becomes an ingrained habit, along with the goals you have set for yourself, and that you review these questions at the beginning and end of each day.

If you think you can do this daily self-question exercise just from memory, please write this down on another card:

The dullest pencil has a better memory than the sharpest mind"

It is impossible to remember all that we know. Until something becomes deeply ingrained as the result of spaced repetition, it is extremely difficult to remember all of the things we need to know at the exactly the same time we need to know them. The 3X5 cards work even when your memory won't. You will automatically move toward whatever you constantly think about just as surely as water runs downhill.

Ask and ye shall be given. Seek and ye shall find.

Brain scientists tell us that we are only using about 10% of our brain's capacity. They may be right. Try this interesting little test and see what you think.

Before going to bed each night, write down one question you would like answered on a pad of paper. Place that same pad on your nightstand beside a good pen or pencil. You will likely awaken either in the middle of the night or in the morning with the answer. That's what the pencil is for. If you do not write the answer down immediately, you may forget it by the time you are fully awake. If you do not get an answer after the first night, repeat the question each night for a week. You will be amazed at the answers your subconscious mind provides if you just give it a chance.

If you persist, this marvelous technique will work for you, just as it has for so many others. Ask one question of importance on as many nights as you would like.

What life-changing questions will you ask yourself today or tonight?

Before you do anything else, write down at least one positive question for yourself right now.

Chapter 8

Action

You will never plow a field by turning it over in your mind.
—Irish Wisdom

Contrary to popular belief, knowledge is not power. It is only potential power. The story of the intellectual derelict is legendary. Only action has the power to create anything. The difference between those who find great success in their lives and those who find life passing them by is the action they are willing to take in order to make things happen for them rather than waiting for things to happen to them.

There are only three types of people in life: Those who make it happen, those who watch it happen, and those who wonder what happened.

If you want greater success in life, you must be or become a person who enjoys making things happen.

Life is like a grindstone. Whether it grinds you down or polishes you up depends upon what you are made of.

Success is not something you pursue. It is something you develop over time. In this process, it is not what you get that is most important. It is what you become. If you choose the path of being a person who takes personal responsibility for making things happen, happiness and success are almost a given. One of the most important questions you can ever ask yourself is "What am I becoming?" What you become determines what you get from life. For the action-oriented person, life's experiences are not the result of random events that most people are taught to expect.

For individuals engaged in self-motivated action, controlling life's outcome isn't random at all. It is destiny by design.

GETTING WHAT YOU WANT

As I stated in the introduction to this book, there really are secrets to easily creating a more successful life. Some of these ideas are already on the list of things you do on a regular basis. Others are things you learned and never got around to doing because you were too busy. Most of them you don't even remember any more. That is because they have gotten lost in the endless details of your everyday life.

To succeed, you must first become the master, not the slave, to habits and outside circumstances. When you become focused, day after day, upon the minute details of daily living, it is a lot like wearing cement shoes: Any hope for meaningful change is slowed down, almost to a dead stop.

The greatest threat anyone has to happiness and success is the tedium of daily living. Getting bogged down in daily habits and "ought to do" busywork means that you are majoring in minor things. This habit is a certain formula for a mediocre life. Most people never find the success they deserve primarily because they become almost totally absorbed in daily busywork.

If you were to drop a frog into a pot of hot water, it would immediately jump to safety. But did you know that if you placed that same frog into a large pot of water and slowly heated the water to a boil, the frog would just sit there until it cooked in its own stew?

I am not suggesting that anyone try this gruesome experiment. I tell you about this well-known experiment to make a point. It is amazing what we can become accustomed to if we are subjected to the slow changes that become the daily humdrum events that fill most of our lives. Now ask yourself this question: Are you now cooking in your own stew?

Doing nothing is a being nothing goal.

The majority of successful people do not usually have more talent than we do; they are just using more of their potential because they have learned they can. They understand that every action or inaction is either a victory or a defeat in the ongoing conflict for our time, and that it is the use of our time that ultimately determines whether or not we win or lose the struggle for a successful life. The major difference between ordinary and extraordinary people is the ability extraordinary people have to get themselves to take action when most others won't. How do they do that? They have developed the unique ability to foresee the future based upon their current actions.

I don't believe that people are lazy. It is just that, unlike highly successful people, they simply don't have compelling goals or the ability to see the future that those goals (or lack of goals) will create. Instead, daily busy work and apathy become deadly killers of their success.

Imagine that two frogs are sitting on a lily pad. One frog decides to jump into the water. How many frogs are left on the lily pad? Two frogs; because *deciding is not the same thing as doing.*

If you want a better life, you must jump into action. While prolonged indecision is not likely to kill you, it will certainly cripple any chance you have for personal and financial success.

Change is unavoidable. Controlling change is optional.

The only cure for apathy is either a dose of passion for a particular goal, or sufficient pain from chronically poor results. Rather than looking for ten reasons *not* to do something, just look for one good reason to do it, and then actually do it.

The fulfillment of our dreams lies not in the distance, but rather lies clearly present within our own hands.

LIFE'S MOST IMPORTANT DECISION

What is your ultimate destiny? What do you want your life to be? Close your eyes, look over last week's events, and see how you used the bulk of your time. Has the use of your time been aligned with the goals you feel are most important?

Now imagine that your daily habits have not changed, and you are ten or twenty years older than you are today. See yourself sitting in the audience of a movie theater showing a movie about your life. At the end of this movie, where do you see yourself living? What is your job like? Who are your friends, and what are they like? Imagine that, at the end of the movie, you are sitting at your kitchen table discussing your finances with someone. What is that discussion about? Is the movie a comedy, a soap opera, an adventure film, a tragedy, or something else? Does your movie have a theme? Is it positive or negative? As you watch the movie, do you want to laugh, cry, boo, go to sleep, ask for your money back, or what?

> *A man is the sum of his actions, of what*
> *he has done–nothing else.*

—Mahatma Gandhi

Another of life's universal rules states that if we fail to change our current habits, we perpetuate any pain we now have in our lives. We may even make it worse. You and I both know that unless you take control of your life with self-directed goals and actions, the movie you have been watching in your mind is very likely to become the real movie of your life.

Take the time right now to write out a list of reasons why you know you must change in order to have a better life. Next, write down what the results will be at the end of the next five years if you do not make each of these changes.

Here is the good news: You are the director, screenwriter, and star of your own movie. You can make it anything you want it to be. It's never too late to rewrite a bad script. When you look back on your real life, what story do you want to tell your grandchildren? What legacy do you want to leave as an example for them to follow? As already noted, the script you get to live will be the result of the goals (or script) you put down in writing, and the actions you are willing or take. Nothing else will be nearly as important as this.

PROCRASTINATION

> *Dost thou love life? Then do not squander time for*
> *that is the stuff that life is made of.*

—Benjamin Franklin

> *Procrastination is the language of the poor.*

Do you know what happens when you give a
procrastinator a good idea? Nothing!

—Donald Gardner

Behavioral scientists tell us that the number one cause for procrastination is our fear of failure. That's unfortunate, because the price of success is much lower than the price of failure. In addition to the fear of failure, many people avoid discovering the secrets to success because, deep down inside, a little voice tells them that the real secret to success is hard work. That's a shame, because that little voice is wrong. Once you change your frame of mind, becoming a success is relatively easy. It is only getting started that is hard. All success is difficult in the beginning. It's a lot like pushing against a giant ball. It takes a lot to get it going, but once it starts moving, the amount of effort necessary to keep the momentum of the ball going is rather easy. So it is with overcoming the inertia of your own life. That first push is the hardest thing you have to do. The more we do, the more we can do.

Many receive advice, only the wise profit from it.

—Publilius Syrus

Did you know that 90% of the rocket fuel necessary to get a spacecraft to the Moon is burned up within the first thirty miles of the trip? Did you also know that after the spacecraft has broken free from the gravitational pull of the Earth's atmosphere, astronauts can go to almost any place in the universe and back on the remaining fuel? All they would have to do is use the gravitational field of each succeeding planet, combined with a tiny burst of energy from the spacecraft's rocket, to slingshot themselves around the planet and onward to wherever else they would like to go.

This example is a perfect analogy for the success methods described in this book. The hardest thing you will ever have to do is to lift off in the direction of your most desired goals. Once you are able to break free of the things holding you back up to this point in life, you will have developed the habits that will take you almost anywhere you want to go with only a little additional boost of motivation at each stage of your journey. When you reach each goal you set for yourself, you will have the additional boost needed to get to the next destination with very little additional emotional effort on your part. When you know you can achieve anything you put your mind to, it becomes fun and much easier. When you know in your heart that you will not fail, it takes almost no additional effort at all. Once you break the grip of current habits and find each success easier to achieve, you will also find yourself choosing all kinds of destinations you once never dreamed were possible. Each challenge then becomes a pleasure, not a burden, to endure.

The best plan is the one you implement.

Procrastination is the thief of time, and time is one of your most valuable assets. In order to succeed, we must first learn to better manage our emotional state. You cannot allow emotions like "feeling overwhelmed" to control your life. This feeling can, and must, be replaced with a daily pattern of activity that helps you break free from procrastination.

An ounce of action is worth a ton of theory.
—Friedrich Engles

If you wait for the right time to get started, you will always be waiting until tomorrow, because there is no such thing as the right time in the future. The right time is always today. There is no limit to the amount of time in the universe. Time is endless, except for the time allotted to you.

Begin doing what you want to do now. We are not living in an eternity. We have only this moment, sparkling like a star in our hand—and melting like a snowflake.

—Marie Beyon Ray

The farmer has no choice but to plow and plant his or her fields to receive any benefit from the land he or she owns. Timing is not something he or she determines. It is dictated by the very nature of the world. Humans, on the other hand, may procrastinate to their hearts delight in the belief that it does no harm to wait to plant the seeds of change tomorrow. The failures of life constantly tell themselves that they are too busy right now, and that there is nothing so important that it can't wait until tomorrow. Just like the farmer, though, if one waits too long to plant the seeds of their desires, the results come to a no good end. No field stays empty, whether we plant it or not. If you do not choose to tend to your own field, circumstances take care of it for you. Unless you are willing to plant the field today with your own possibilities, and the seeds of our own desires, your field will eventually be filled with weeds.

TIME LIMITS

Even if you're on the right track you'll get run over if you just sit there.

—Will Rogers

If you are not willing to set time limits on your goals and take these time limits seriously, then you are not serious about finding greater success and happiness in your life. If that is the case, please take this book into your back yard and dig a hole. Then gather your family and friends around you and mourn together for your future success. Then you might as well bury this book deep in the ground along with your chances for future success. Don't kid yourself that this or any other book can help you, because without goals and time limits, you are not going to change.

Goals without deadlines are just wishes. Wishes are dreams of reward without effort. Having goals without deadlines is not how success happens. Wishes alone will get you nowhere. To have the results you want, you must set deadlines for each and every one of your goals. If you do not, your subconscious mind will know instinctively that you are not serious, and it sabotages whatever efforts you do make.

It is not necessary to have your time limits chiseled in stone. You will always have the option of taking whatever extra time you need once you are over the first couple of hills and on the way to your goal. As you make progress, your new abilities and your vision of future possibilities will become clearer. Your initial time limit may be too optimistic, but it is better to be too optimistic than it is to underestimate your ability. Remember: we tend to live up to our own expectations. If you set your expectations too low you may just achieve them. It is far better to be aggressive in the time limits you set, and perhaps arrive a little bit late, than it is to make it so easy that it does not challenge you to grow into the new person you want to become.

Once you set deadlines for your goals, something powerful happens. You realize that you now need some sort of plan. You also realize that the distance between your ultimate goal is not one giant leap, but rather a series of steps. If you wanted to eat an elephant, you could do so. You just couldn't do it in a single day. You would have to accomplish this goal over time, and so it is with all your big goals. In order to be successful, you must first break your big goals down into a series of smaller goals and time limits. With that in mind, start by first setting a deadline for completion of each big goal. Next, list the small steps you want to accomplish within the next week for each big goal. Now, before you go to sleep tonight,

103

take a few minutes to write down on a 3X5 card the most important goals you want to accomplish before the end of the day tomorrow. Begin tomorrow and each succeeding day in this same way.

A journey of a thousand miles begins with a single step.
—Chinese Proverb

It is not necessary to figure out all the steps in advance that you will need to get you from where you are to where you want to be. It is only necessary to get yourself pointed in the right direction and to start moving along the most obvious path. Depending upon the nature of your goal, some of the steps you must take in the future will not become obvious until you are a long way down the road. They are not important right now. All you need to carry this out initially is the first few steps. The best pathway to follow in the future will reveal itself to you as you move along. In fact, many paths you cannot now imagine will suddenly open up as you move further and further along the path of progress. There is a special magic that presents itself each step of the way. That magic is called *opportunity*. *Opportunity* always presents itself to those who are alert and moving in the direction of a meaningful goal.

ACTIVITY MANAGEMENT

What a folly to dread the thought of throwing away life all at once and yet have no regard to throwing it away by parcels and piecemeal.
—John Howe

I know you are busy. We all are. Life is complex. It seems that there is never enough time, but each of us has all there is. If you are serious about increasing your chances for success in the future, you must somehow find ways to set aside time each day in your schedule for the goals that are important to you. We know that one of the keys to a happy life is a feeling of being in control. Control only comes from taking the time necessary to move us in the direction of our goals. If you do not grasp the helm of your own life and actively steer in the direction of your own most desired results, don't expect some magical force of nature or human kindness to do it for you.

Time is the most valuable asset we have. The supply is severely limited. There is only a small and uncertain allotment made available for each life. Unlike rare gems or money in the bank, we cannot store it away for later use. We cannot give it away or buy it. We can only use it wisely or unwisely. The only control any of us has over time is how we use it. If you cannot maintain control of your activities, you cannot maintain control of your life. If you desire a happier life, you must learn to align the use of your time with the goals you set out as important to your own success. All intelligent time management requires planning because there actually is no such thing as time management, there is only *activity management.*

The best way to free up a time slot for your important goals is to take a short time in the very beginning to develop more effective ways to structure your activities. Planning first and acting second is usually the most time efficient way to reach any goal.

Life is short, and one of the best ways to use the time of your life is to copy the best ideas of others. I make no claim of authorship to the following ideas. Like so many of life's lessons, they are the practical accumulation of a lifetime of seeking out better attitudes and ways to manage my own time. I find each to be helpful, and I trust you will as well.

1. You will never find extra time for anything. If you want time, you must schedule a time slot for it to appear. This applies to relaxation as well as work.

> *Time is nature's way of making sure everything*
> *doesn't happen all at once.*

2. Activity management is your way of making sure that at least something that you want happens.

> *Don't be fooled by the calendar. There are*
> *only as many days as you make use of.*
> —Charles Richards

3. Buy a daily calendar that can sit on your nightstand. Before you go to bed each night, tear out the page for each day and tell yourself, "There goes another day of my life. It will never return. Today I have spent one of my most valuable assets." Then ask, "Have I spent it well?" This exercise will not allow you to take your time for granted.

> *You will never catch a rabbit if you chase nine at a time.*
> —Chinese Proverb

4. De-junk your life. What now exists in your life that could be better organized? Do you save too much paperwork, or have ineffective storage and retrieval methods? How many hours of your life are you willing to spend shuffling through piles of disorganized things at home or at work to find something you know is in there somewhere? Is your correspondence with others handled in priority order, such as by placing it in A, B or C piles? Do you handle pieces of paper more than once rather than making a decision immediately upon reading it and moving on to something else? Do you plan your activities in advance so you can go from place-to-place or chore-to-chore without unnecessarily backtracking? Do you schedule time to think and work without interruption? Starting today, change those habits that leave your life cluttered, inefficient, and bogged down.

5. Learn to say no without guilt. This is the time of your life you are spending. Are you letting the priorities of others take control of your life? I am not suggesting you stop contributing your fair share to the betterment of your family, friends, or humanity in general. It is wonderful to be helpful and nice to others, but even being nice must have limits. Do your best to schedule the requests and demands of others in ways that allow you the time you need for yourself. You do no one any good by being constantly frustrated and overburdened with the problems of others.

6. Take a speed-reading course in place of some of the time you would normally use up by watching television.

7. Use your normal drive time more effectively by listening to audio recorded lessons or motivational talks and books on tape. Your car can become your time efficient, rolling university if you will let it.

> *Take care of your minutes and the hours*
> *will take care of themselves.*
>
> —Lord Chesterfield

The day can be divided into 24 hours, 1,440 minutes, or 86,400 seconds—the choice is yours. If you choose to think in terms of minutes and seconds, it is clear there are plenty of times during your daily activities that you are not using to your best advantage. The question now becomes, "How do I find those inefficient time gaps so that I can take advantage of them?" Here is the answer;

8. Write down, on your *To Do* list, to buy a small note pad you can easily carry, and then add a deadline to complete this chore. Starting the moment you get this notepad, record everything you do during the day and how long you spend at each activity. Do this exercise for no less than one week, including the week-

end. Until you do this exercise, you will not know where your time is actually being spent. Remember, this is the time of your life you are spending. Be sure that you are spending it in ways you think are best for you. Otherwise, you are robbing yourself of your most precious asset by your own inattentiveness. Ask yourself this, "Is there a high or a low payoff for the way I use the limited time of my life today?"

9. Carry a *To Do* list with you at all times.

When I first learned of this idea, I was told I would accomplish ten times more in my life if I kept a written list of all the things I wanted to do. I discovered this assumption was not the truth. In fact, I estimate I have accomplished at least a hundred times as much as I would have otherwise.

You probably already have a *To Do* list, either in your mind or on slips of paper you keep somewhere in the house, or maybe on your iPhone or Blackberry or the calendar on your refrigerator. What I am talking about, however, is a different method that can make all the difference. I am talking about a more inescapable arrangement. I am talking, once again, about the humble 3X5 index card.

I favor a 3X5 card method because the cards are easy to carry in a purse or shirt pocket wherever you go. They are also inexpensive, and easy to rewrite and replace. You can do a daily *To Do* list on just one side of a single card, and individual cards are easily rearranged as your priorities change.

Do you do first things first? By that, I mean making a list of the three most important things you would like to accomplish each and every day. Once you do this, set a starting time and do not let anything else interfere until these three things are completed.

This technique is not just about work. Since real success also requires relaxation and playtime, this technique also applies to the pleasures of life you wish to enjoy.

Take out the 3X5 cards where you previously wrote your goals. Choose the one goal you feel most passionate about. Write down at least one action that to complete today to move closer to completing that goal. Set a time limit for its completion sometime today. Now, do not go to bed before you have fulfilled this promise to yourself.

Do these exercises every day with at least one goal. When you do, you will find certain success, because taking daily action is like having a turbocharger attached to the dreams of your life.

Daily action is the fuel your turbocharger needs to drive you towards each of your goals, as fast as you would like to go. Instead of feeling overwhelmed, you will feel energized by keeping your mind focused on positive goals and the action plan for their attainment

Don't overlook the advantages of delegation. One of the best ways to maximize your results is to delegate at least some of your goals and activities to others. Delegation is not something you can do with your happiness goal, but it is often possible with other types of goals. Maybe that means sharing chores around the house with your spouse, or the kids to give you more time to read. Maybe it means you hire others to do work for you rather than spending your time becoming a master of do-it-yourself techniques. Since delegation is such a good technique, why not start activity management effectiveness training by sitting down and making a list of anything you might be able to delegate to someone else?

If you are willing to implement the ideas listed above you will find that you really can accomplish far more than you ever imagined.

Using activity management techniques to your best advantage does not mean you should feel stressed and driven to be productive in every waking moment.

Life is a journey, not a destination. Success is therefore ultimately measured by what you become and how deeply you can appreciate and enjoy the moments that constantly flow from the fountain of life.

This discussion of activity management is intended to encourage your participation in re-examining some of the time you currently allow to slip past you on a daily basis and for no good reason other than inattentiveness. Therein lies the opportunity for significant advancement toward your most important goals.

*The shadow by my finger cast, divides the future
from the past. Behind its unreturning line,
the vanished hour, no longer thine.
Before it lies the unknown hour, in darkness and
beyond thine power. One hour alone is in
thine hands. The now on which the shadow stands.*

—Wellesley College Sundial Inscription

Chapter 9

Habit

The true nature of the brain is misunderstood, and therefore, the process of positive change is usually far more difficult than it otherwise needs to be. Neuroscientists tell us that, contrary to popular belief, the brain is not a magnificently coordinated, one-piece unit designed to handle all situations with equal efficiency. The brain has instead developed in very different layers and stages over millions of years. Each layer is designed to serve specific purposes existing in the environment of the various stages of our evolution.

Anthropologist and neurophysiologists estimate that the brain we are born with today is the result of an evolutionary process that has taken about 500 million years, give or take a few million years. Neurophysiologists have learned relatively recently that we do not have a single decision making brain, but instead a multi-level brain with each brain layered one on top of the other. First we have the brainstem, the oldest brain. This brain is very similar in appearance and design to a crocodile's brain. The next brain evolution provided is the limbic brain. It evolved to manage body temperature, thirst, food intake, and weight maintenance. The limbic brain is also responsible for most of our primitive physical and emotional reactions, such as our body hair rising up when we are cold or frightened. The final and largest brain to evolve was our cerebral cortex. The cortex's two hemispheres give us the right-brain and left-brain thinking differences that we have all heard about. It is responsible for the art and science that fills our world. It is the repository of all of our rational, contemplative thinking.

Each of our three brain sections has a specific purpose and talents. To add to the evolutionary confusion, each of these brains also *has a mind of its own*. While one brain may focus on alertness for danger, the second brain may suddenly get our attention to judge the weight of a grapefruit. Seconds later, the third and most highly evolved brain layer may suddenly decide to interrupt to solve the meaning of life or some less weighty problem. Because of the multi-layered, overlapping nature of our rational and non-rational brains, it is impossible to be totally focused and rational at all times.

The true nature of our mental focus is not focus at all. It is a constant mental switching back and forth between different brain systems and various combinations of talent centers within each brain. Even though our brain stem and limbic brain autonomic and emotional systems seem to run on autopilot, they still manage to interfere with the thinking of our cortex's right and left hemispheres. That is why, even when we try to maintain concentration on a particular subject, we still frequently find ourselves drifting off course and completely lost in intervening daydreams and thoughts on entirely different subjects. Staying completely focused on one train of thought all of the time is virtually impossible. It is this multi-faceted nature of our brains that is always an obstacle that must be overcome on our way to reaching any new goal we set for ourselves. However, where there is a will, there is a way.

I am your constant companion.
I am your greatest helper or your heaviest burden.
I will push you onward or drag you downward to failure.

I am completely at your command.
I am easily managed; you must merely be firm with me.
Show me exactly how you want things done, and after a few
lessons, I will do it automatically.
I am the servant of all great men and, alas, of all
failures as well.
I am not a machine, though I work with the precision of a
machine plus the intelligence of a man.
You may run me for profit or run me for ruin; it makes no
difference to me.
Take me, train me, be firm with me, and I will put the world
at your feet.
Be easy with me and I will destroy you.
Who am I?   I am habit!

Habits make you or break you. Like it or not, unless a catastrophe or some other shock to our normal habit pattern intervenes, each of us functions almost completely on autopilot—all day, every day. Which sock do you put on first? Which side of your face do you start shaving or put your make- up on each morning? Do you ever stop to think about it? Have you ever taken the off-ramp to your job instead of the road to home, or some other destination, simply because you weren't thinking, and habit made the decision for you?

Back when having excellent fight or flight instincts meant you got to live or die, there frequently wasn't enough time to carefully weigh all incoming data our senses provided before making choices. Therefore, our evolutionary journey in the survival of the fittest provided each of us the ability to filter out most repetitive sensory data of normal, daily life. That information is simply stored in our mental databanks as background information.

We have evolved into beings that focus our attention primarily on new information our senses detect as sensational, unusual, and perhaps immediately important to our well-being. Then we use a combination of intuition and shortcut thinking to decide what action, if any, we should take. We do this because we would be overwhelmed if we stopped to give every decision well-reasoned and rational thought. Our mind is constantly creating new beliefs and habits with this ancient process to survive drowning in the ocean of sensory input data constantly flooding our awareness.

Despite all of the progress we have made as we evolved out of the oceans, came down from the trees, and into our fine, modern houses, the deepest levels within our sensory systems still work pretty much the same as they did millions of years ago. We still run pretty much on habits and instincts dictated by our past evolutionary process. While habits and instincts have, no doubt, saved our skins time and time again throughout mankind's march to civilization, they have also limited us in many ways. One of those confining barriers occurs when they get in the way of our willingness to test the limits of what we think we can achieve or become.

To a certain degree, a mouse in a maze exhibits more intelligence than some human beings. If a mouse doesn't find the cheese after a number of tries down a particular path, it will eventually try another path. Most humans will go down the same path in life forever because habit and instinct tell them it is the "right thing to do."

I'm not suggesting you should abandon your natural instincts, even if you could. I am, however, suggesting that if you want to achieve superior results with your life, it requires more than your existing habits and instincts. It requires systematic, spaced, repetition to overcome old habits and create new, more effective ones. We cannot escape our ancient nature, but each of us still has enormous potential to more fully utilize rational thinking techniques in order to maximize our success in life. That is because success is not an all-or-nothing game. It is a matter of degree. Multi-brain thinking and habits are obstacles each of us can overcome, if we choose to do so. It simply requires that we have a rational method that can be systemically followed in order to help us remain more consistently focused on the changes we want in our lives.

SPACED REPETITION

We are what we repeatedly do. Excellence then is not an act, but a habit.

—Aristotle

Spaced repetition is the mother of all new skills. It does not matter whether you are learning to walk or learning a foreign language for the first time. Until new information is deeply embedded in the synapses of your mind, you will be unable to perfect your new skills and repeat them with ease. We do indeed become what we repeatedly do.

If you are to change the person you are now, you need to change some of your current habits. Since habits are mind/body memories that are deeply ingrained within your rational and irrational brains, they are not easy to change. If we are to overcome our old habits, we need to have very specific, clear, new thought patterns ingrained by new repetitious patterns of thinking and activity.

No matter what else you do in order to succeed, you must incorporate the tactic of spaced repetition to assure that the necessary consistency and the persistence is not lost as days move into weeks. Therefore, take at least five minutes, twice each day, for the next 60 days to center your thoughts. Serenely and peacefully visualize your goals as you would like to see them fulfilled.

It will take a minimum of twenty-one days of spaced repetition before you can expect to change any well-entrenched habit. This time frame is based upon what is known as the "phantom limb syndrome," which is a common experience for amputees. After a limb is removed, the brain may still produce pain which it identifies as coming from a limb that no longer exists. This usually continues for up to up to twenty-one days. This is the power of habit in your mind. Your limb may be gone, but your brain refuses to accept that fact for typically at least twenty-one days. This resistance to change is also true when trying to remove, replace, or alter any of your current habits.

Until you begin experiencing the long-term results achieved by using consistent repetition and never-ending persistence, you cannot possibly imagine how much potential for achievement you actually have. No one in my high school graduating class (including myself) would have been willing to bet you five cents against five hundred dollars that I would write this book; I can assure you of that. My English teacher would not have wasted even a penny on such a bet. I tell you this only to impress upon you that you do not know the limits of your possibilities until you decide to persist in the pursuit of your dreams.

Educators tell us that different people learn more or less effectively depending upon the methods we use. Some of us learn best by utilizing our visual memory. Others do best when they are taught lessons orally. Still another person may learn best by writing and re-writing new information on paper. Despite the differences in effectiveness between these various methods, one thing is clear: We all learn best by involving every sense we have. Therefore, if you want to change a habit more quickly and effectively, combine all three of these techniques with spaced repetition.

Once again, I find that 3X5 cards are the best way to stay consistently on track with clear, consistent thinking and actions. They work just as effectively as the flash cards you once used at an early age in school.

Let these cards be your guide in whatever you do; they will not fail you. First, form a clear picture in your mind of the action or goal you want to achieve. Now, think about every aspect of that picture as you write down a concise description of that goal. Read this goal aloud to yourself twice a day as you vividly picture the final result in your mind again and again. In time, this goal will become a part of your subconscious mind, and you will soon begin to think of many different ways it might be accomplished. You will also soon understand what to do next.

This technique works if your goal is to not do something, like smoking, but be sure you never state a goal in negative terms. You don't want negative goals in your life. It is far more effective to reframe *don't want* goals into positive *do want* results. For example; Replace "I don't want to smoke anymore," with "I have quit smoking because I want to live a happier, longer life. I want food to taste better, and I expect to enjoy the power that controlling my own habits gives me."

Notice that I did not suggest "I will try to quit smoking." There is a world of difference in being willing to *try* and just quitting. If you stop smoking, even for a day, you are not trying to quit, you have quit. Once again, the message you give your conscious and subconscious mind is very important. If you want to stop doing something, you must first decide if you are stopping or just trying. If you are just trying, you might as well not start because you have already decided that it is okay to fail. That is not the kind of winning attitude that will get you what you want.

If you are determined to persist until you win, you will win far more times than you will lose. Winning is almost inevitable if you refuse to quit. It is just a matter of spaced repetition, time, and persistence. The only way you can fail is if you quit trying. Winning is about never giving up.

SELF-AFFIRMATIONS

Just like the importance of internal questions you ask yourself, the messages you repeatedly give yourself in the form of internal verbalizations are also vitally important to your happiness and success.

What you say to yourself repeatedly will eventually manifest itself, as surely as the sun rises and sets each day, no matter where you are in the world. That makes written, mental, and vocal self-affirmations critical to your success. Any unhelpful habit you wish to change requires a new message to replace the one you are now giving yourself to support your bad habits.

For example: What if you were now lying to yourself by constantly telling yourself something like, "It's OK to eat large portions of fried foods all of the time, because my extra weight and body fat are just not that important to my health and fitness. Besides, it tastes good, and that makes me happy, so I don't care what people think.

If you wanted to lose weight, replace that internal message with something like, "I am proud of myself because I enjoy eating only the right foods in the right amounts necessary to reach and maintain my peak health and physical fitness. That makes me feel good."

Without a new internal message playing over and over again to replace the unhelpful, prior message, the current habit will not change. After a while, the new message is not one you need to practice repeating. It becomes part of the new person you are working to create. You will enjoy exercising and eating the right foods in the right amounts, and you will not even remember what it was like to have the unhelpful habits of the past. You will become a better you, and you will be happier and proud of yourself. Your self-esteem and self-confidence will soar with each new success in changing old, unhelpful habits.

Self-affirmations are a time-tested way to instill new discipline without the emotional struggle and pain typically encountered when you try to change an old habit through plain grit and determination. When positive self-affirmation is added to a written plan of action, and repeated daily over long periods of time, change becomes almost automatic. Your mind eventually absorbs the new message as the new truth. It then becomes true, as your old habits give way to positive, new change. It also becomes easier and easier with each practice and new success. These new and positive messages support and encourage the state of mind ultimately necessary to succeed in whatever goal you set for yourself. With self-affirmation and self-discipline, habit change becomes quite easy, and you feel much happier about the new you that you created.

The best way to replace old, unwanted messages with new and better ones that support the change of habit you want is to first write it down on paper. Choose a time each day to set aside to read and repeat this new self-affirmation aloud at least twenty times each day for at least a month. As you repeat it aloud each day, you will find you refine the wording to exactly the right phrasing to fit yourself perfectly. This is not difficult to do. The best time to do this is at the beginning of each day. In that way, the affirmations support and encourage you to do the right thing throughout the day, every day.

Although regularly using self-affirmations does not guarantee you don't backslide on some of your achievements, that is not important. What is important is to continue using affirmations until they are deeply ingrained in who you are and how you want to be. Eventually, you will reach the goals you want for yourself. Just keep telling yourself that "it is not a question of if, but when."

DON'T STOP UNTIL YOU SUCCEED

Failure usually follows the path of least persistence.

After you create a list of steps to immediately take as part of your short-term action plan, list the intermediate time frame mileposts you plan to reach along the way to your final destination. These mileposts are the evidence you need to show yourself that your progress is constant, even if it is not as fast or as consistent as you expect.

When you reach these mileposts, hold a party. Even good habits benefit from reinforcement. It is time to celebrate your progress. Efforts without reward are no fun at all. Treat yourself (without guilt) to something special.

Chapter 10

Responsibility

IF IT'S TO BE, IT'S UP TO ME.

For most people, lack of control is at the very root of a great deal of unhappiness. Gaining a sense of control over your own destiny is, therefore, a very important and necessary ingredient in any formula for lasting happiness.

Having a greater sense of control is powerful medicine. Self-confidence eventually flows from this feeling of control. Ultimately, this ever-expanding self-confidence becomes the foundation upon which all of your future successes are built. Those successes also become a continual source of optimism. How and where does responsibility fit into this picture? It is not the word itself, but rather how you use the word that matters most.

I love the word "responsibility" because, whenever I think of this word, I think of two separate words: response and ability. My definition of responsibility is: "The ability to respond in the manner I choose."

In fact, I alone choose the response I have to whatever life presents at my doorstep each and every day of my life. That is because I choose not to have a knee-jerk reaction selected for me by someone else. I decide what response is best for me. You can choose to do the same if you wish to begin the practice of doing so. Living in a free country automatically grants each of us the right to this marvelous gift. We simply have to choose to use it.

Destiny is not a matter of chance; it is a matter of choice.
It is not something to be waited for; it is something to be achieved.

—William Jennings Bryan

If you approach your life based on the recognition that you are in control of all of your responses to life's challenges, you will truly be the Captain of your own ship and master of your own destiny.

The perfect analogy is that of the ship's Captain, who says: "I cannot control the wind, but I can adjust my sails. I can sail any course and reach any destination I want, no matter what direction the wind is blowing."

Like that Captain, you can also choose to adjust your sails and steer whatever course you choose for your own life if you choose to take control of your ship's wheel. Grabbing the wheel is done by using your *response - ability*.

If your ship doesn't come in, swim out to it.

—Jonathan Winters

Responsibility, therefore, is not a burden to be carried, but rather the gift of self-determination. It is the crown jewel of all attitudes. Best of all, it is free for the taking, and no one can ever steal it from you without your permission.

When someone insults you, how will you respond? Will you respond by lashing out in anger? Will you respond with graciousness or cleverness? How about forgiveness? How about responding with pity and forgiveness for their ignorance because you understand they are the one who is ultimately punished by society because of their own poor personality and attitudes?

Will you use their insult as an opportunity to demonstrate the sterling quality of your own gentle, loving, generous, and thoughtful character, or will you choose to show them your lack of personal control? It is a choice only you can make, and make no mistake about it: Learning how to shape your response in the manner you choose determines the direction of your life.

With practice, you can learn to adjust your response to every event life hands you in ways most beneficial to reinforcing the values, attitudes, and actions that determine whether or not you become the person you wish to be. If your goal is to constantly become a better person, each response you make to life's daily moments is of great importance. Even when life hands you disappointments, you have an opportunity and a choice of responding in a way that continually moves you forward in the direction of becoming a better you.

Having the goal of constantly taking responsibility for becoming a better you always pays big dividends in personal happiness and satisfaction. There is great comfort in simply knowing that, although you are not perfect, you are constantly polishing your personality to the greatest extent you can.

Since exercising your *response - ability* in a careful and thoughtful way is the key to your every success, it is well worth taking time to practice using this new skill. You cannot change the world or anyone else in it. However, with practice, you will have much more control over changing yourself.

The amazing thing about self-change is that when you change, so does the world around you.

When you are turned down for a job you wanted, how will you respond? If you fail an important test, how will you respond? If you only reach 80% of a goal you set for yourself, how will you respond?

At each junction of action and reaction in life, there is a choice to be made. It is your responsibility to use your *response- ability* to choose the most positive and productive response possible in order to create a constantly improving and better you. It is not difficult. It is simply a mindset that chooses to recognize that you are, in fact, in control. Only you can choose to make things happen for you, rather than allowing yourself to end up wherever someone else's tide or wind forces you to go. Where do you want to go?

TELL YOURSELF THE TRUTH

In this process of taking control of your life, it is very important you learn to never lie to yourself. You owe yourself a higher standard than that. Trial and error is the foundation of all progress, and you are responsible for some mistakes. When you are the cause of poor results, don't lie to yourself about it. When it is your fault, don't look to shift part or all of the blame to someone else. There is much to be gained by not kidding yourself about who is responsible for your mistakes. It simply does you no good to point the finger of blame at others for your failings. Being honest about your own weaknesses is the first step along the road to making positive changes that are of great benefit to you later on.

Don't lie to yourself or try to cover up your shortcomings. There is nothing quite as refreshing as someone who admits openly that they were wrong, or those who admit that they need and would appreciate help from others.

At times, this can be a very tough rule to follow. Whenever the human ego is involved, there are many opportunities to violate this critical rule of self-examination. Those who perpetually ignore this rule usually pay a very dear price at some time in the future. Objective insights about yourself can be very helpful if you will not get overly defensive with yourself. Knowledge, especially if it is about yourself, is power.

RELAX

Relaxation is another response you can train yourself to choose. You will find it to be very helpful if you learn to *really relax* at least once, preferably in the middle of the day, for a minimum of fifteen minutes.

The greater the calmness of our minds, the greater our peace of mind becomes. The greater our peace of mind becomes, the greater our ability to enjoy a happier and more joyful life.

Unless you have already learned at least one of these skills, consider making it one of your goals to take meditation, self-hypnosis, or yoga lessons. If you agree that this is important, why not set a deadline for completion of that goal right now. Decide right now upon a time today when you will make whatever calls are necessary to find out more about one or all these techniques of self-empowerment.

These techniques not only help to create greater emotional stability and happiness, but they are also frequently useful in dealing with physical pain. Learning these techniques also helps you to sleep longer and awake more refreshed.

You will discover you can think more clearly than you now do. With practice, you will also find yourself and your thoughts more energized, and you will be better able to take advantage of more of the positive opportunities that are available every day.

Chapter 11

Relationships

Thousands of books have been written on the subject of human behavior, and no short chapter can possibly hope to cover all the worthwhile concepts useful to your goal of happiness. Nonetheless, no book on the subject of happiness would be complete if it did not address human relationships. Unless there is a good measure of harmony between you and the people important in your life, you are very unlikely to find much happiness. Sooner or later, we all discover that relationships are what matter most.

Almost everyone would agree that when a home burns, and once all the people and pets are safe, the next most important thing to try and save are photos containing the pictorial history of family and friends.

The philosopher Aldous Huxley once said, "There is only one question of importance, and that question is, 'Who am I and what, if anything, can I do about it?'"

While it is important to your self-determination and happiness that you seek the answer to that question, it is equally important that you ask if there is anything you can do to better understand and relate to other people in the world who affect your life. Ultimately, your happiness is directly related to the results you help create.

THE FOUR LEVELS OF HUMAN RELATIONSHIPS

There are basically four different levels of human relationships that affect your personal happiness level. They are: self, world, family, and couples. In your pursuit of greater happiness, it is worth your time to examine each of these relationship levels in greater detail.

SELF

During any honest, introspective examination of yourself, it's helpful to remember that each of us starts out, at birth, demanding something from others. It is a necessary survival instinct, and usually serves us well. This inward, self-centered view of the world, as well as our needs, expectations, and the demands we often make of others, persists throughout our adolescent years. For some, it may persist far longer. When it does, it is usually very unhealthy and detrimental to one's personal happiness.

Up until this point, this book has been about the self and the things you can do to be the best person that you can be. We have already recognized that working towards improving your own skills and attitudes is the surest and shortest path to happiness. However, as you continually move toward that goal, it may seem that others are not as helpful in your quest for happiness as they could be. In many cases, the relationship problems you believe are intentionally caused by others are not. They are simply a difference of personal, biological, or cultural value systems and our own interpretation of events that involve them and us. When you think others are wrong, always remember this:

Nothing has any meaning except that which you give it.

As part of our *mastery of self* goals, most individuals benefit by including the goal of achieving a much higher degree of understanding of human differences that tend to cause conflict and drive us apart.

THE WORLD

The most basic ingredient to all positive human relationships is mutual respect. Contrary to popular belief, respect is not necessarily something that must be earned. Rather, it is something that can be freely given—as one component of unconditional love— once our natural differences are more closely examined and understood. We do not live in a world of black and white or right and wrong. Rather, it is a world containing every shade of every color in the rainbow. There are no good colors or bad colors; there are only different colors. Other than the motives of greed and evil, almost all other human struggles are about clashes of understanding and values.

Without a larger global perspective, it is difficult, if not impossible, to appreciate the true beauty held within the wide variations of social styles, value systems, and behavioral biology at play in the background of each human. Without a more global view of the world and your place in it, compassion, understanding, tolerance, and respect for others is not very likely to materialize on its own. Without more flexible attitudes and perspectives, open, honest, and more caring relationships are not likely to be created or allowed to grow.

Whenever I think of human relationships, I am reminded of the story of the three blind mice asked to examine an elephant with their hands and explain what they find. As I recall the story, the first mouse approaches the elephant and finds its leg. He explains that the elephant is very much like the trunk of a tree. The second mouse finds the tail and disagrees. He explains that an elephant is like a rope. The third mouse finds the elephant's massive side, and explains that both of the other mice are wrong, because the elephant is obviously like a very large wall.

Since each mouse's opinion is based upon undeniable truths, each mouse is fundamentally right about its facts. Each is still absolutely wrong regarding the true nature of that elephant, however. While few of us are quite as handicapped as the three blind mice in understanding and explaining other people and our relationships with them, we could, nonetheless, all use some help in one way or another to better understand the endless variety of complex interactions of human beings.

The mind is like a parachute. It works best when it is open.

Most relationship difficulties are not caused by bad intent, but rather by less than ideal levels of understanding of what it truly means to walk a few miles in the other person's moccasins.

In our journey of greater global understanding, it is helpful to start with *The Golden Rule* as an example. Every culture in the world, at least that I am aware of, has some version of "Do unto others as you would have them do unto you" rule. While the intent of *The Golden Rule* is to do things to please others, there is an inherently flawed assumption built into the rule. Within this rule, it is assumed that if you do what you think is a good idea, everyone else will appreciate it just as much as you. Unless you and the recipient of your efforts share exactly the same value systems, the appreciation you expect as a result of your effort may never occur at all.

The problem occurs largely because of the fact that everyone does not think as you do. Therefore, we individually fail to appreciate that everyone else in the world has not learned and adopted the values and judgment systems we use every day to determine wheth-er or not things are fair, right, unjust, improper, correct, dignified, tasteful, funny, stylish, inconsiderate, or anything else. Therefore, we cannot sometimes appreciate that others are not necessarily inconsiderate, stupid or anything else just because their culture, religion, gender, or experience causes them to view the world and respond to it in very different ways. To the extent that you lack appreciation and respect for the endless variety of individual dif-ferences, you will find personal harmony and happiness all that much harder to come by.

To be truly happy, you must generally and genuinely like people. This does not require that you attain the level of unconditional love displayed by Jesus or the Dalai Lama. The closer you absorb and practice the teachings of any of those practitioners of un-conditional love, the greater your own happiness will be. On the other hand, the less you respect and appreciate individual differ-ences, the more difficulty you will have acquiring a wide circle of friends—even a mate. Additionally, the relationships you do de-velop during your lifetime will be more superficial, strained, and more difficult than they need to be.

Imagine what you would be like if you were born into an Eskimo family located far above the Arctic Circle. What would you consid-er "normal" food? Would you consider a mixture of blubber and blueberries a dessert? Would it bother you to kill seals, fish, whales, or arctic birds to put food on the table? How would you feel about never stopping at the coffee shop for a doughnut or another sort of treat? What would your political opinions be? What would your religious views be, if any? Who would you consider a good choice for a marriage partner, and how would you determine that? What qualities would you find attractive in the opposite sex? Would hair-style or lipstick color matter? Would you plan to go to Florida in the wintertime?

What would your life be like if you were born into a poor farming family in North Korea? What would you be like if you were born into a rural tribal family in a war-torn part of Africa?

Now imagine that you were born in Calcutta, India. How would you like someone in Calcutta to do unto you, as they would have you do unto them, in accordance with their social and religious customs? Human lifestyles are amazing and fascinating in their diversity, but only if you can truly respect and appreciate such differences.

In the wonderful melting pot of countries around the world, variety truly is the spice of life. Each of us has the opportunity to make an unlimited number of friends, but only to the extent that we can hone our relationship skills through a broadened appreciation and respect for both the obvious and the subtle differences that make every one of us unique and special.

FAMILY

He's not heavy; he's my brother.

When we talk about family, we must also include our extended family, comprised of friends and associates. Normally, anyone within this family circle receives special consideration simply because they are known to us on more intimate levels than *just strangers.* Even though we don't always agree with all of our family members, we usually defend them from insults or the abuse of others, unless they are extremely abusive or hurtful themselves. Sometimes we defend them even though we know they are not good people. Frequently, we choose to forgive them for their faults, and forget their mistakes even when they are abusive simply because they are *family.*

We do so because we feel a special bond of understanding and/ or appreciation that does not naturally exist with outsiders.

Despite this family bond, there is no guarantee of harmony and happiness. Irrespective of each family's level of cohesiveness, flexibility, or supportiveness, there is always a certain amount of disagreement and tension. Disagreements vary widely over time. Most tension and turmoil has to do with the conflict between the roles we play out with each other on the stage of life and how we communicate.

Our happiness is always subjected to the test of rules we did not make and family members we did not get to choose. Therefore, the degree of flexibility and adaptability each family member has eventually decides whether these relationships are happy ones or not. Whatever the dynamics happen to be within your family, you will always have an opportunity to play a positive role. The greater your knowledge on this, the greater the chance relationships will improve.

Are any family members going through life playing the role of the "martyr," or perhaps "Cinderella"? How about the role of the strong, silent, "hero-type," or maybe the "helpless wife"? Maybe your family includes the "Angel of Mercy," or even a "devil in blue jeans." Perhaps you or those around you are playing, "Now I've got you," or "Ain't it awful," or "Poor me," or "I'm only trying to help," or any one of a hundred other games people play consciously and unconsciously every day.

It has been said that, *understanding the problem is 90% of the solution.* That old quote has never been truer than when it comes to creating and maintaining happier relationships with those around us. Whatever role you and those around you play, you need more than just hope or luck to change relationships. A good understanding of the dynamics of those roles and the ability to recognize the needs of each individual playing those roles is critical in the process of helping create positive change. A good starting point is to simply objectively observe that games are being played. With this knowledge, you will be far better positioned to participate with, or withdraw from, relationships that do or do not work well together.

FRIENDS

Sometimes you just can't make a silk purse from a pig's ear. I have heard it said that we choose our friends as compensation for the fact that we cannot choose our relatives and the members of our families. The ability to choose one's own friends is a great gift that should not be taken lightly. If you wish to soar with the eagles in life, first be sure you do not choose to hang out with a bunch of turkeys.

If you do not find the love and support you need within your family or current circle of friends, it can be very helpful to accept the fact that you cannot change others. You can only change yourself. The relationship responses you receive from others are, to some degree, a reflection of your own action or inaction. Therefore, it is important you learn to see the causes and effects in relationships, and seek to make changes as necessary in your own life to get you to where you would like to be.

Whatever your current situation, if it is time to change the dynamics of your relationships, first you must recognize and understand the games being played. If you now experience problems because of the way people treat you or try to manipulate you or the ones you love, there is a book you should not be without. That book is *Games People Play,* by Eric Berne, M.D. This famous book, first published in 1964, continues to sell well after all of these years because of its classic lessons regarding family, friends, and the behavior patterns of couples. Even if you think there are no games played within your relationships, I am confident you will find this wonderful book very useful in helping you see and understand many of your interpersonal relationships much more clearly. With this new insight, you will be prepared to become a better person, which will, in turn, create better relationships.

INDIVIDUAL STYLES

In addition to the roles and games people play, there are more subtle differences in individual style that are not as easily recognized or understood. A common problem each of us must solve every day is how to better understand and communicate in ways that are clear and helpful to all the partners in our lives. Even when we have the best of intentions, without clear communication, we often feel hurt, rejected, or confused, to say the least.

In attempting to better understand and communicate with others, you may seek to unlock the answers to various personality questions by exploring your own and others' innermost feelings and thinking. Theories regarding how to create and maintain good human relationships abound. An individual's personal theory about human behavior may emanate from many places. They may come from various aspects of psychology, astrology, tarot cards, the Psychic Hotline, the large universe of magazine articles available, and, of course, the help of friends.

While some answers to individual style and personality may lie in those kinds of explorations, most people only deceive themselves if they believe they find definitive answers by looking there. Using these methods, you have only a small chance of actually figuring out what makes people respond in the ways that they do.

The solution to your problem may lie not in your ability to understand the inner person, but rather, your ability to simply observe the outer person on display in front of your very eyes.

The famous Greek physician, Hippocrates, outlined four human temperaments; Sanguine, Phlegmatic, Melancholic, and

Choleric. Many others since his time have noted specific personality types as well. Most notably, the famous Swiss psychologist, Carl Jung, first wrote about *archetypes* in 1921, in his well-known effort to explain the variations in human personalities. From his works, we have come to know such words as *introvert* and *extrovert*. Jung labeled his four archetypes: Intuitor, Thinker, Feeler, and Sensor. Since his work primarily focused upon people seeking help in resolving significant psychological problems, he spent little time exploring the various psychological personality types displayed by ordinary people.

Many years after Jung's work, Isabel Myers and her mother, Katherine Cook Briggs, undertook the task of combining Jung's work with their own to develop it into information more useful for lay people to evaluate and understand. The result of their historic work was first presented to the public in 1943. Today, about 2.5 million people each year take the Myers-Briggs Type Indicator personal inventory test.

Most who take this test do so as part of a job application or aptitude test done for *the benefit of someone other than their- self.* Even though they are exposed to the Myers-Briggs concept, they are usually never able to use this test to better understand their interactions and inter-relationship dynamics with others.

In *Gifts Differing*, Isabel Myers Briggs explains the ideas and concepts behind the Myers Briggs test and the sixteen social attributes most people display. Knowing this information surely helps if one of your goals is to better understand the actions and reactions of those around you every day.

Two additional works are also particularly noteworthy. They are the best books on the subject I have ever found.

The first is *Personal Styles and Effective Performance,* by David W. Merrill, Ph.D. and Roger H. Reid, M.A.

The second is *The Platinum Rule,* by Tony Alessandra, in collaboration with Michael J. O'Connor.

The format within Tony Alessandra's book is very similar to that of David Merrill's in that it draws in part from the research first done by David Merrill in 1964. Hence, these two books, although different in their various observations, are clearly cut from the same cloth. The differences are basically the names applied to the four personality styles and each author's individual suggestions on how to use this knowledge.

If you have not yet read either of these books, I cannot tell you how thrilled I am to introduce them to you. That is because there is a very strong possibility that they will very quickly change your relationship skills for the better. In so doing, they create many opportunities for positive change your life.

What follows is a very simplistic sample of the basic concepts contained within each of these exceptional books. Upon reading and applying the full information and wisdom contained within each book, you immediately broaden your understanding and appreciation of those you choose to like or dislike. With this new insight, I guarantee that you will find you suddenly have a far greater capacity to understand and communicate with those who you may have found difficult or confusing in the past.

THE PLATINUM RULE

Tony Alessandra's book, *The Platinum Rule,* is a welcome derivation of *The Golden Rule.* The Golden Rule states, "Do unto others as you would have them do unto you." The Platinum rule states, "Do unto others, *as they would have you do unto them.*" In order to follow *The Platinum Rule,* one must first have the capacity to recognize and understand what the other person would *appreciate you doing unto them.* The beauty of Tony Alessandra's book is that, to a large degree, it allows you to do just that.

Theorists of many backgrounds have attempted various ways to classify differing personalities. These different models have used everything from the names of birds and animals, to even colors, to label these personalities. The most common thread throughout the centuries, however, seems to be four basic types. That is also the number Tony Alessandra (top row, below) and David Merrill (bottom row, below) have chosen to use in their work. Their four personality style types of both authors are:

a- Director	b - Socializer	c - Relater	d - Thinker
a -Driving	b - Expressive	c – Amiable	d - Analytical

Obviously, style labels alone are of little help in improving one's ability to understand and relate in more positive ways with any-one. What is needed is a graphic explanation. The examples that follow are very similar to the methods used by each of these fine authors. Since these very short examples cannot hope to convey a total understanding of this subject, my hope is that, after this short introduction, you are motivated to learn more by reading the ac-tual books in question. Used copies are available online for only pennies more than the shipping costs.

To begin your journey understanding the field of personality style, let us begin by first thinking of someone you know who has a con-versational style of asking, rather than telling, when they want you to do something. Most likely, that someone also has an indirect, rather than a direct, way of asking for help or information. When you think of that person, how would you rank them on the scale (below) from 1 to 20, with 1 being *asking indirectly*, and 20 being *telling or demanding?*

Asks   1-2-3-4-5-6-7-8-9-10-11-12-13-14-15-16-17-18-19-20   Tells
Indirect   Direct

Now think about this same person and try to place him or her on a scale of emotions and sensitivity 1 to 20. Does he or she express a lot of emotions and feelings, or is that person cool and collected with their feelings at all times? Are the decisions he or she makes based primarily upon facts, or are decisions more likely based upon feelings? Is that person happier when socializing with people, or not? When you think of him or her, how would you rank this person on an emotional sensitivity scale, from 1 to 20?

Governed   Controls
by Emotions   Emotions
&   1-2-3-4-5-6-7-8-9-10-12-13-14-15-16-17-18-19-20   &
Feelings   Thinking
Oriented   Oriented

As you can see, it isn't usually that difficult to give a relative rating to the way people around you act out their lives. Although no individual is exclusively one way or the other at all times, one dominant style is often evident. Let's go one step further and create a matrix of style variability that better reflects how the two scales can be used to create four basic style possibilities relative to each other. To see how this concept works, assume the person you thought about scored an 18 on the *ask/tell* line, and a 7 on the *emotional* line. Their dominant style would be that of an *Expressive/Socializer.*

Emotional

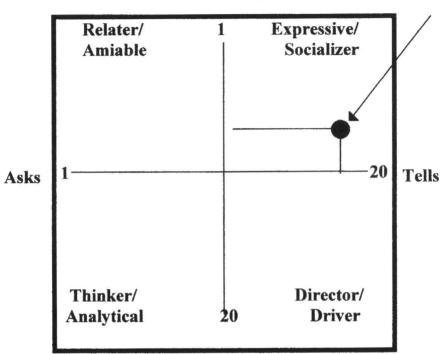

| Relater/ Amiable | 1 | Expressive/ Socializer |

Asks | 1 ——————————— 20 | Tells

| Thinker/ Analytical | 20 | Director/ Driver |

Controlled

To avoid any confusion about what each style means, let's take a little time to add a few more descriptive adjectives to each of the four different styles. By doing this, you will find that you will automatically begin to think about who might match each particular style.

The Amiable or Relater: This person values relationships and feelings above all else. Family and friends are often the focal point of this person's life and activities. This person cares a great deal about how others feel about him or her, is sensitive to others, and enjoys learning all about them. This person usually asks questions indirectly. This person has many family pictures, enjoys long conversations about people, and is deeply hurt when relationships fail. This person enjoys being supportive to others. Oprah comes to mind.

Thinker or Analytical: This person is able to control or suppress their emotions more so than the Relater. When making decisions, this person requires lots of data in the decision-making process, and usually makes decisions slowly. This person thinks facts are more important than gut instinct and intuition. This person appreciates great detail and a structured environment. This person actually reads the instruction book, and knows how to operate all of his or her electrical devices. An accountant, engineer, or computer whiz may come to mind.

Expressive or Socializer: This person could have been the class clown. This person is not bothered by clutter and disorganization. This person enjoys adventure and risk. This person enjoys brightly colored clothes, and loves to entertain others with music, art, or literature he or she created. Being spontaneous and imaginative are the hallmarks of this person. Robin Williams may come to mind.

Driver or Director: This person enjoys being in charge, is very good at organizing meetings, and keeping things running smoothly. This person is usually in a hurry, and is task-oriented. This person is comfortable delegating responsibility, and only wants a summary of key facts to make a decision. Does your boss or Donald Trump come to mind?

I could go on and on, but it is not my intent to cover every aspect of each style. That would take an entire book. However, we can take a look at how we might get a further sense of where someone belongs within each dominant style box.

Since nobody is completely one style or another, we must think about subdivisions within each of the four quadrants of the style boxes. Those subdivisions might look something like the illustration below. Let us see where the person used in the previous example ranks within the sub-style boxes.

(Relater)		(Expressive)	
Amiable	Expressive	Amiable	Expressive
Thinker	Director	Thinker	Director ●
Amiable	Expressive	Amiable	Expressive
Thinker	Director	Thinker	Director
(Analytical)		(Director)	

If you are the extreme *analytical-thinker* type, you probably realize you can also now subdivide each of the sixteen sub-style quadrants by four and have sixty-four style subdivisions. If you are *not* predominately the analytical type, I am sure you will find the last illustration sufficient without further refinement.

If you are not the *analytical* type, you will be happy just understanding how picking a number from 1 to 20 on the horizontal *Ask - Tell* line, and then selecting the appropriate number on the vertical *Emotions - Controlled* scale you can quickly arrive at a sub-style within the dominant style box that most fits the person you are trying to better understand.

When thinking about people according to their social style, it is also important to understand that you can find both good and bad individual attributes in every style. Whether or not the person who fits any given style acts in ways that are either good or bad is ultimately a matter of character, which has nothing at all to do with their social style—just as there are no good or bad colors in a rainbow, and there are no good, bad, better, or best social styles. If you think about it, you soon realize that you know good, bad, successful, and unsuccessful people who easily fit into each of the four possible social styles.

There is another method you may also find useful in classifying a person's social sub-style. To use this alternate method, simply decide which style is the most dominant or obvious for a given person. Next, assign a percentage number to each of the four sub-quadrants within the most dominant style. For example, you may think of someone as belonging predominantly in the *Expressive* quadrant. Upon thoughtful reflection, you may then decide that, within their dominant style, they are 10% *Expressive*, 15% *Amiable*, 25% *Thinker*, and 50% *Director*. If you observe closely, you will notice that in different situations, this person emphasizes one style over the other, but eventually they always revert back to their dominant style.

WHY IS THIS IMPORTANT?

The ability to understand other people in this way is important because, to the extent that you understand what is important to others and the manner in which they communicate their thoughts and feelings, you can now begin to apply T*he Platinum Rule,* rather than T*he Golden Rule.*

You will also understand how they communicate has less to do with *who you are,* and a lot to do with *who they are and their personal style.* If a person's intentions toward you are to create an enjoyable relationship, you now have a far better opportunity to understand what they mean based upon how and what they say—even if they do not communicate their intentions in your own preferred style.

If you think about it for a moment, you will realize that o*ught to* and *should* are almost always terms that *apply to your style and values*, and not necessarily to the values and styles of others. That is, of course, unless you believe your way is the only valid way in this world.

If you have a disagreement with someone you care about, or if you feel offended or put off by the way someone expresses their thoughts to you, it is extremely helpful if at least one of you can better understand that differences in personality styles may be what gets in the way of better relationships. Just because someone does not think or act in the same style or with the exact same value system you do, it does not automatically make you right and him or her wrong.

When individuals experience difficult times, it is wonderful to recognize and appreciate the ways each of us is different, and to be able to accept those differences in a spirit of understanding. In that way, you have a far greater opportunity to be empathetic to whom they are. You can, at least, agree to disagree and still remain friends.

You may still be frustrated or impatient when you interact with someone whose style is much unlike your own. With practice, you will find that thinking in terms of the various style quadrants, you will become far more patient and capable of actively listening and interacting with others ways that both of you more fully understand and appreciate. All relationships that work well are based, in part, upon good communication. You have the opportunity to apply this new knowledge toward your greater happiness.

Being happy does not mean you have found a way to make every person or everything perfect in your life. It does mean you have found a way to see beyond imperfections, which are always bound to exist in an imperfect world. The following is a good example of what I mean.

COUPLES

Men Are From Brooklyn: Women Are From Paris

The man/woman idea expressed above is not be nearly as amusing as it is to most of us if it were not for the fact that it contains more than a small element of truth. Beyond the obvious differences between males and females, there are numerous opportunities for conflict and anguish of one kind or another.

> *Love is all you need.*
>
> —The Beatles

If a man from a city in China married a woman from a rural tribe in the Amazon rain forest, it does not take a genius to figure out that they will need a lot more than love or lust to make their relationship work. This clash of cultures could cause unlimited opportunities for disharmony. What is less well-understood or appreciated is the fact that much smaller differences between couples also can cause big trouble. You need more than love to maintain a satisfying male/female relationship.

Marriage is one of the most complex of all human relationships. Joining of a male and a female in a relationship intended to last a lifetime is guaranteed to have happiness problems that need resolving. A clear demonstration of that is the U.S. Census Bureau's report of 2.4 million marriages and 1.2 million divorces. This same report estimated that nearly 20% of all marriages fail before the third anniversary.

Marital satisfaction studies conducted over the last twenty years clearly show that relationship satisfaction can be expected to significantly decline in the first two to three years of marriage. Much of this decline is the direct result of unrealistic hopes, expectations, views and beliefs held prior to the marriage. This is quite predictable, since very few pre-marital couples successfully anticipate the number and types of conflicts they encounter.

Even though it is gratifying to know that marital dissatisfaction does not always result in failure, it is a clear indication of the need to find satisfactory ways to resolve conflicts between men and women that every marriage entails. Adding children to the equation makes things even more difficult.

Research shows that, although happiness stabilizes around the four-year mark, it normally declines again at about seven years. In fact, *the average length of marriage in the United States is only six years*. This is partially due to the normal re-examination of one's role and goals undertaken as we mature. Another contributing factor is the lower quality of the marital relationship couples often experience during the child-rearing phase of their marriage. Beyond those causes, however, the inability to resolve most conflicts in a win-win way is still the major cause of marital failure. What the statistics tell us is self-evident. Most couples are not well prepared to deal with the unforeseen challenges every marriage inevitably brings.

Clearly, to have happy relationships, it is necessary to do more than just have mutual respect for regional, cultural, and family differences. The top two components for a happy partnership between a man and a woman are just what you might suspect: better communication and flexibility. This means that if we are to find greater happiness, we must learn more effective ways to communicate and receive thoughts and feelings in ways we fully understand on a *meta-linguistic* level. Being skilled in meta-linguistic communication requires having the ability to communicate where the person receiving the message understands the meaning of the words almost identical to the way it is understood by the person delivering the message. Let's assume there are three men talking about what it is like to be afraid of dying. Let us further assume that one of the men has never been in a life-threatening situation, while the other two have been in nighttime combat together with bullets and rockets landing all around them as they hugged the ground and prayed be alive at daylight. The two men understand meta-linguistically a real fear of death. The third man does not. It is the meta-linguistic communication between men and women that is virtually impossible. Thankfully, communication skills can be improved with desire, training, and positive effort, and can go a long way to enhance mutual understanding and respect for each person's true nature. Prior to undertaking this effort, however, there is much to be gained by reflecting upon even a few of the fundamental differences between most men and women. Remember, this is not a witch-hunt. We are not looking for faults or flaws. We all have enough of those without trying to attach any such meaning to the general social and biological characteristics of men and women worldwide.

PREDISPOSITIONS

It was not that long ago that men and women required much more of our brawn and wits than we do today to simply survive on this planet. Some of our characteristics are obviously biological, while others are learned socialization skills emanating from our biological predispositions, and blended with social survival skills. Some of our stronger tendencies worth considering are as follows:

Please recognize these simplistic stereotypes as exactly what they are: overly simplistic to make a point—nothing more

Predispositions	Male	Female
Survival strategy	*brawn*	*brains*
Territorial response	*attack*	*defend/negotiate*
Dominate hormones	*testosterone*	*estrogen*
Hormone fluctuations	*low*	*high*
Aggressiveness	*high*	*low*
Communication	*direct*	*indirect*
Decision-making	*independent*	*consensus*
Social goals	*freedom*	*family*
Income producing	*mandatory*	*secondary*
Child-rearing role	*subordinate*	*dominant*

Although each of us may demonstrate more or less ability to move away or toward the standard stereotypes, by and large these gender-related roles and predispositions are remarkably universal worldwide. Clearly, there are easily defined gender differences that exist between most men and women. The list could be longer or shorter, but the point is simply this: There are differences we cannot change in our chosen partner. Therefore, we would be wise to enter our relationship of unconditional love expecting compromises and changes that we will not be completely happy with at first (and maybe not even later). Rather than focus on the differences (real or perceived) in a search for solutions, it is far more productive to search elsewhere for answers to the age-old question: "How do we more perfectly bond with our chosen mate?"

The answer, assuming that *real love* exits in the first place, in large part lies in a greater understanding of, and clearer communication on, the differing needs and points of view of each partner based on social value systems and individual social styles.

Greater understanding and flexibility is a *joint effort*. Even though the effort is very unlikely to be an equally enthusiastic effort on the part of each individual, it can still bear wonderful fruit.

RATIONALITY

There are basically two ways that normal people deal with the variables that life offers each of us, in ever-increasing amounts, the longer we live.

The ways are either rational or emotional. To be more exact, they are some combination of the two. The only question remaining is the ratio of these factors one uses in dealing with life's many problems and opportunities.

By themselves, either choice, or any combination of the two, work perfectly as long as there is never more than one person involved in any particular situation. One would only need to do whatever makes them personally comfortable in each and every situation. The problem arises when two or more people attempt to work together to deal with life's situations. Here are the reasons why.

The extremely rational person (analytical-type personalities) usually steps back emotionally from each situation to first gather, organize, and examine facts to reduce complexity to the most efficient and manageable decision-making level deemed necessary to avoid mistakes and thereby achieve a successful outcome, without regard to any emotional consideration.

The highly rational person often finds satisfaction and enjoyment by solving, complex problems. This rational process is frequently a source of personal self-esteem and success. Because of this approach to life, others often incorrectly characterize this person as cold, unfeeling, and insensitive.

The extremely sensitive and emotional person (relater-type personalities) usually attempt to make decisions and take action based on whatever tends to make them feel more emotionally comfortable and secure. This often involves reducing complexity and conflict in favor of simplicity and certainty. Uncertainly is unusually disturbing and worrisome to this person because a sense of possible danger and unwanted results are a constant source of worry that easily disrupts their desire for security and personal comfort. Because other people's opinions and feelings are so important to the highly emotional person's own sense of well-being, the process of dealing successfully with others is frequently a source of personal self-esteem and success. Because of this approach to life, others often incorrectly characterize this person as friendly, but foolish.

I hope you take particular note of the fact I used the term *extremely* emotional or rational. I stress this because extremely emotional or rational people are in a special category by themselves. It is almost impossible for such people to ever work successfully together. Thankfully, most humans have a good portion of both emotional and rational decision-making propensities. Once again, we are back to a matter of degree.

Let's assume for the moment that one person conducts life with a 20% rational and 80% emotionally driven process, and they are involved in a problem-solving situation with someone that conducts life with an 80% rational and 20% emotionally driven process. As you can imagine, this is not an easy process. One or both of these individuals will have to make a substantial compromise in their personal behavior pattern preference to reach a solution. It is nice to realize that we, if fact, do have a degree of flexibility, rather than a fixed amount of emotional or rational decision-making capabilities. However, to make this joint problem-solving situation even more complex, the more important the decision-making situation becomes, it is usually the case that each of these individuals move more toward their dominate trait or "comfort zone," rather than away from it.

These observations are not about right or wrong. They are simply about human nature and what makes different people comfortable. Ultimately, what each of us does is what makes us most comfortable—even if that action is to compromise to reach an agreement.

The predominately emotional person will never be completely comfortable with a predominately rational decision-making process, and the predominately rational person will never be comfortable making a decision based upon a predominately emotional decision-making process.

There is strong evidence that suggests that the imperfect ratio of rational to emotional behavior and decision-making is a major cause of disharmony for men and women attempting to build a life together. If recognizing the problem is truly 90% of the solution, then perhaps these observations, even in this simplistic example, will help.

Perhaps all men are predominately from Brooklyn, and all women are predominately from Paris. Each of these locations has good and bad qualities. How you feel and your comfort level with each of these places depends on your perception of each, rather than on the actual location.

BLISSFUL COMPROMISE

When asked if their relationship experience agreed with the following statements, the following is the percentage of individuals in happy and unhappy relationships who agreed.

	Couples Survey Report	*Happy Couples*	*Unhappy Couples*
1	I am satisfied with how we talk to each other.	90%	15%
2	We are creative in how we handle our differences.	78%	15%
3	We feel close to each other.	98%	27%
4	My partner is seldom too controlling.	78%	20%
5	When discussing problems, my partner understands my opinions and ideas.	87%	19%
6	I am completely satisfied with the amount of affection from my partner.	72%	28%
7	We have a good balance of leisure time spent together and separately.	71%	17%
8	My partner's friends and family rarely interferes with our relationship.	81%	38%
9	We agree on how to spend money.	89%	41%
10	I am satisfied with how we express spiritual values and beliefs.	89%	36%

The preceding list is the result of research done over the past twenty years, as reported in the wonderful book by David H. Olson and Amy Olson, *Empowering Couples: Building on Your Strengths*. (Also consider *The Couples Checkup* book.)

David Olson's work first began as an exploration of couple dynamics and the predictability of marriage success or failure. Subsequently, more than 50,000 professionals have been trained using his methods. More than a million couples have taken the *PRE-*

PARE/ENRICH test designed by David and his associates. These tests and courses are now widely available throughout the country. While there are many worthwhile books that explore specific solutions to specific problems couples encounter, David and Amy Olson's book is a very good beginning on the road to understanding how to become a happier couple.

While it is always helpful to do what you can on your own to improve your communication skills, you may find this quite difficult without some guidance and a lot of consistent practice. Unless you can learn to make permanent additions to your conversational style—such as "This is what I understood you to say. Is that what you meant?"—you may significantly decrease your odds for lasting relationship happiness by not seeking some form of outside help, such as the *PREPARE/ENRICH* course or similar training you may find available where you live. If any of your conflict resolution discussions contain phrases such as, "The trouble with you is..." run—don't walk—to one of these sessions.

In most human endeavors, it pays big dividends to first understand others before you make yourself understood. Better communication skills, when added to a high degree of non-judgmental love, surely helps. The rewards you receive for the effort you make in this area of your life will astonish you with the amount of happiness and success you receive in ways you never imagined possible.

Better relationship skill building is not a zero-sum game. No one has to lose in order for you to win. Win-win relationships are the kind that last. Along the way, they also grow and enrich the lives of all parties involved. None of us will ever achieve perfection in our attempts to be the best we can. However, it is the efforts you make in that direction that are the stepping-stones to your current and future happiness. It will not happen all at once. If it did, it would deprive you of the enjoyment and happiness you are destined to experience along the way, as you continue to grow into a wiser and better you.

Chapter 12

Persistence

Nothing in the world can take the place of persistence. Talent will not; nothing is more common than unsuccessful men with talent. Genius will not; unrewarded genius is almost a proverb. Education will not; the world is full of educated failures. Persistence and determination alone are omnipotent.

—Calvin Coolidge

As with all the best-laid plans of mice and men, you will have problems. When they occur, it is best if you have developed a strong sense of self and a determined attitude that simply accepts failure as a natural part of the growth process. Each of the preceding chapters has given you a good start to understand how to map your dreams, lay out a plan of action, and change unproductive habits and beliefs. If you have the benefit of genius, natural talent, or a good education, you are truly blessed. No matter what your circumstance may be, to succeed, you need a path to follow and attitudes you can adopt and adapt with persistence over time. To accomplish that result, you will need to have a clear outline of the things that matter clearly etched into your mind.

IN SUMMARY

1. Nothing changes until you do. Happiness is a choice, and it starts with you. It is a state of mind rather than a slave to events. Happiness needs to be renewed each and every day. It rarely lingers in the presence of those who do not have a positive attitude and an attitude of gratitude.

2. You need to have a dream to make a dream come true. Dreams and wishes without an action plan are a source of frustration, not happiness.

3. Put your goals in writing; be specific. By doing this, you will be in the top 3% of individuals who take control of their lives and actively steer their destinies in the direction of their goals rather than letting circumstances steer them. A life without goals is like a ship without a rudder.

4. A goal without a deadline is a message to your subconscious mind that it is okay to fail. Thought without action is like a car without gas.

5. Procrastination is failure on the installment plan. There is only one right time to start, and that is now. Life is already too short. Every day is a precious gift; don't waste it.

6. Never aim for low goals, or that is all you will achieve.

7. We all have obstacles to overcome, but you are a unique person and have (and can further develop) unique talents no one else will ever have.

8. Think big, but start small. You can escape the trap of low self-esteem and low expectations by adopting the *Kazen* method of continuous, small-step success. By using this method, you

will soon learn that you can do anything you put your mind to. Over time, you will learn that you *do have* what it takes to achieve the life you want for yourself. Over time, you will not *think* you can reach your goals—you will *know* that you can.

9. Approximately 98% of everything you do is the result of habit. When you change your habits, you change your life. The easiest and surest ways to change old habits is to adopt strategies that promote systematic, spaced repetitions on a daily basis. The best method for doing that is a simple 3x5 reminder card to use for your written goals, positive motivational quotations, positive and productive daily questions, and your daily *To Do* list. Use your 3x5 cards for daily review in order to stay on track. Without them, you will forget 97% of everything you have read in this book within a few days.

10. Visualize yourself in the future as you would like to be. Your subconscious mind will take this new visualization message as a directive to start fulfilling your vision of yourself. After visualizing your future goals, you will find that your subconscious mind will come up with many suggestions and ideas of how to achieve dreams that you had never considered before.

11. Take responsibility for your own happiness and your successes or failures. Develop your *response-ability* so that you can control your responses to circumstance, rather than having circumstances control you. Attitude is everything. It is not how things are but, rather how you see them that determine if you are happy or a failure.

12. To succeed, you will need systematic positive reinforcement. Search for the stories of wonderful people whenever you read. You will find them if you look. Find positive people to associate with. Avoid listening to negative junk news and television programs. Remember, garbage in means garbage out. You deserve

better than that. Buy (or borrow from your local library) motivational material such as CDs, DVDs and positive idea books on a regular basis. If you use them, they will make all your days happier and more productive.

13. Build strong, positive relationships by increasing your communication skills and staying on an optimistic and positive track, regardless of what circumstances come your way. The best way to change others in a positive way is by becoming a better you. You can do that by better understanding who they are and what they need rather than by understanding who you are and what you need.

14. Adopt a goal of life-long learning for continued personal growth. According to recent neurological research, your mental capability actually grows as you increasingly use you mind. You can become a far greater success than you ever dreamed. You can because that is what thousands of others like you have already done with these same techniques.

15. Follow the *KIS* rule. (*Keep it simple.*) Things will be much easier to remember and follow if you learn to reduce complex ideas into the essence of their meaning. That is why thoughtful quotations are so helpful. Over time, you will find that you become better and better at remembering what is important among the endless clutter of information. Doing so is called wisdom.

16. Be persistent. Don't let setbacks stop you. When things get difficult, hang in there. Refuse to quit. The gap between reaching your goals and failing is usually much smaller than you think. If you refuse to quit, you will never be a failure.

With the power of spaced repetition in mind, let me suggest that you write each of the summary items down on individual 3X5 cards and review each of them daily until you are able to repeat at least part of each one of them to yourself and to others without looking at the cards.

A LIFE WELL-LIVED

A life lived well is art of the most beautiful kind. It is a rare gift to yourself and those who share this planet with you.

- It is a balancing act between fulfilling your personal needs and fulfilling the needs of the world around you.

- It is maintaining the delicate balance between the discipline of personal responsibility and the need to find daily humor and happiness.

- It is having the strength to help yourself and those around you when times are most difficult.

- It is having character and integrity that gives you the strength to act appropriately when others may not.

- It is having an excellent value system to live by.

- It is having sufficient belief in your own abilities so that you can largely control your own destiny.

- It is most often measured by the number of positive relationships you are able to build and sustain with mutual enjoyment throughout your life.

To the extent that this book has helped you accomplish some or all of these goals, be very proud of your accomplishments. You have earned and deserve them.

If you wish to share your experiences regarding this book the author would be pleased to hear from you at;

creatingthegoodlife@yahoo.com

Made in the USA
Charleston, SC
24 June 2014